PRAISE FOR
BUILT WITH PURPOSE

"They say that sometimes it's easier to communicate complex ideas by telling a simple story to get your message understood. *Built on Purpose* is a beautiful business story about an outrageously successful company called Torch Technologies. In reading the book, I found myself thinking about how and where this team of people developed the instincts to make the decisions and moves they made to be where they are today.

A totally unexpected job loss by the founder, Bill Roark, set him on such a comeback that Bill never forgot the pain and suffering of that loss. Bill also made a mental note to never let it happen again; not only to him but not to anyone who worked with him. A mental note like that becomes an instinct you can use to build a company from the ground floor up knowing fully well that failure is not an option. You need to have a Plan B or C if you are going to engage the lives and the futures of the people you work with.

I found myself reading between the lines of the story to understand the beauty within. It was the 'Takeaways' that I picked up that made the story truly valuable. The employee-owners of Torch did what they did because they wanted to build a community of businesspeople who not only wanted to do good for each other, but also for the communities where they lived, played, and prayed. What's remarkable is the ripple effect created by the founders and employee-owners of Torch. Not only did they create wealth, but they also figured out how to distribute it back to the people as equally and safely as possible.

They collectively built a business of collaborators and decision-makers while also establishing contingencies to cover for any chance of an economic downturn. And all along the way they never forgot to be grateful to the cities, counties, and countries they live in.

This is a book about *instincts* influenced by learning and experience. A set of *instincts* that were developed by taking risks, taking on responsibilities, and caring about one another. This is a compelling story of not only one person but the power of a collaborative mindset. It proves that if you plan out far enough together, while also addressing the questions that prevent you from getting there, your chances are that much greater that you will make it to where you want to go as a business.

This is the story of Torch, a company that has set an example of why ownership is so powerful and why more of it is needed now more than ever."

—Jack Stack, President and CEO of SRC Holdings

"Bill Roark's remarkable work to make Torch Technologies one of the most admired and successful companies in its industry, its community, and in the world of employee ownership is an inspiring and instructive tale of how much can be achieved when you truly empower people and share their success with them."

**—Corey Rosen, Founder of the
National Center for Employee Ownership**

BUILT WITH PURPOSE

How Our Employee-Owned Business Changed What It Means to Work and Why

BILL ROARK

WITH DARREN DAHL

River Grove
BOOKS

Published by River Grove Books
Austin, TX
www.rivergrovebooks.com

Copyright © 2024 Roark Publishing LLC

All rights reserved.

Thank you for purchasing an authorized edition of this book and for complying with copyright law. No part of this book may be reproduced, stored in a retrieval system, or transmitted by any means, electronic, mechanical, photocopying, recording, or otherwise, without written permission from the copyright holder.

Distributed by River Grove Books

Design and composition by Greenleaf Book Group and John van der Woude
Cover design by Greenleaf Book Group

Publisher's Cataloging-in-Publication data is available.

Paperback ISBN: 978-1-63299-802-6

Hardcover ISBN: 978-1-63299-803-3

eBook ISBN: 978-1-63299-804-0

First Edition

CONTENTS

Acknowledgments

Every book written about a defense contractor like Torch Technologies needs to include a thank-you along with a debt of gratitude for the service of our soldiers. Our goal has always been to give our warfighters the best machinery, equipment, and weapons they need to complete their missions and return home safely and with their bodies intact. We should never forget the enormous sacrifices these men and women make to maintain the freedoms and principles of this country for all of us. God bless each and every one of you.

I also need to give special thanks to all our government and military customers who have trusted and believed in the Torch family for more than two decades. We continue to appreciate the relationships we have built over the years and strive to deliver outstanding value to our customers while serving as good stewards of taxpayer money.

There would also be no Torch without the support of the Huntsville community at large. Thank you for all the support you have given us over the years. That's why continually giving back to our community through donations of time and money is such a vital part of our company culture.

I also owe a note of thanks to Roy Nichols and Chris Horgen, the cofounders of Nichols Research. Roy and Chris gave me the opportunity to blossom in my career while also inspiring me with a vision of what a truly employee-centered culture could look like. Don Holder and I started Torch using the lessons we learned from our years at Nichols.

The story of Torch is much more than mine to tell. I am so grateful for the many members of the Torch family who gave their time to share their experiences and, in some cases, to help me remember what really happened over our first two decades. First among them, of course, is Don Holder, to whom I owe an ocean of thanks. I learned so much about business and the art of working with customers from Don. He will always be like a brother to me.

I also need to give special thanks to Clay Hagan, Joe Hill, Scott Parker, John Watson, Steve and Janet Haenisch, Clayton Newkirk, Sue Clark, Debbie Overcash, Tina Corley, Terry Thomas, Brad Walker, Dave Cook, Cindy Walz, Brady Porter, Charlie Crowe, Corey Chandler, Ben Phillips, Amanda Clark, Brenda Conville, Lee Holland, Jaye Bass, Anita Wood, and many others—especially other Torch employees who gave their time to make this book a reality. This is your story as much as it is mine.

Thank you also to the friends I have met over the years who helped inspire our journey, like Corey Rosen from the National Center for Employee Ownership, writer Bo Burlingham, Jack Stack of SRC Holdings, and Dave Whorton from the Tugboat Group.

But I also owe a debt of gratitude much closer to home. Without the unerring love and support of my wife, Brenda, and my two daughters, Amy and Kaitlynn, I wouldn't be here today. The same is true for Torch and the writing of this book, neither of which would have been possible without my family's support. I love you all dearly.

I'd like to thank Darren Dahl for his help in channeling my words and stories onto the pages of this book. I've enjoyed our collaboration, and I like to think I've made a friend along the way.

And finally, I am thankful to my entire family, especially my parents, Charles and Ruth Roark, who taught me to respect others and instilled a great sense of right and wrong into me. Together, they were a rock, and their guidance left me a great compass for doing the right thing. I also thank my brothers and sisters and their spouses, who were all much older than me. But they often guided me with additional parental advice. I love them all dearly. I especially owe a great deal to my oldest sister, Marcella Mullins. She invested much of her time in educating me about things beyond Leslie County where we grew up and always pushed me to move forward, even today.

Foreword

You might say that Torch Technologies, the company founded by Bill Roark and Don Holder in 2002, took off like a rocket, which would be particularly appropriate given its location in Huntsville, Alabama, birthplace of the American space program and home of the NASA US Space & Rocket Center. It grew so fast that it soon began spinning off other fast-growing companies—little rockets, so to speak. As Bill Roark explains in these pages, the point came when he realized Torch needed a parent company to watch over all the rockets, and so he founded one that he called Starfish Holdings because of the starfish's ability to regrow an arm when it loses one. A starfish is thus built to survive, as he intended Torch to be.

There is a story about starfish that seems germane in this context. It involves a man walking along a beach and coming upon a boy who is throwing things into the water.

"What are you doing?" the man asks.

"I'm throwing starfish back into the ocean," the boy replies. "The surf is up, and the tide is going out. If I don't throw them back, they will all die."

The man laughs. "You know there are miles of beaches here and hundreds and hundreds of starfish. You can't really make a difference."

The boy listened politely and then bent down to pick up another starfish, which he threw into the ocean. "It makes a difference to this one," he says.

Bill Roark's starfish are the people of Torch Technologies and its sister companies. He may not be able make a difference in the lives of all the working people in America, but he has already made a huge difference in the lives of the men and women who work in the companies he created. If all entrepreneurs did the same, they would light up the world and change the way we understand the power of business and the promise of capitalism.

—**Bo Burlingham,**
author of *Small Giants* and *Finish Big*
September 2023

The Torch Story– Keeping the Dream Alive

T his is the story of the founding and growth of Torch Technologies from a two-man shop into a significant defense services firm. It is my story, as well as that of my cofounder, Don Holder. I am generally an optimist, so the pages of this book focus on the positive developments that made Torch successful over its first twenty years. Torch is not a utopia, but it is an incredible place to work because our culture is unique. From the very beginning, we were founded to be an employee-owned company. Every current employee who has been an employee for ninety days and is employed on the last day of the year has beneficial ownership in the company.

This book is also about friendship. Torch is a special place where you can work together with people you respect and whom you like as friends. The journey to build this company has had many hurdles along the way. Those challenges were made easier because of our culture of cooperation and, in almost all cases, genuine friendships. It isn't that conflict hasn't existed along the way. But we came together to overcome it. It made us stronger; it made our products for our customers stronger. Ultimately, it contributed to our shared success.

Please note: Our employee-owned culture motivates our employees to work together to positively drive the success of our company and support our customers. Working together is encouraged and rewarded. With that spirit in mind, this book generally avoids negatives (like stories of our internal conflicts and bickering, which were minimal compared to other organizations where I've worked) and instead focuses on the accomplishments that led to our success.

To understand the importance of the story of Torch Technologies, you must first look at what we have accomplished. The company just celebrated its twentieth anniversary. We did it with great fanfare, as we usually do for big events. We had a celebration party and a cookout where we enjoyed barbeque, hamburgers, and hotdogs prepared on the company's giant grill (bought years ago for company celebrations like this). We had prizes of all sorts. While it was our normal way of celebrating, we took it to a grander scale. Perhaps more importantly, it was a time to reflect on everything we had accomplished over the past two decades.

One of the things I am most proud of is the commitment

to the community our employees have continued making through Torch Helps, our award-winning, employee-run charitable giving organization, as well as the direct support that's come from the company itself. Since our earliest years in business, we have been well known for supporting our community of Huntsville. For instance, we pledged a $20,000 grant each month to charity in celebration of our twenty years in the community. And we will greatly exceed that amount this year, as we have many times in the past.

Torch has been a very blessed company, greatly exceeding any goal or expectation Don Holder and I had set when we opened the doors. We never dreamed we would build a company that would grow to this size or be heralded with so many awards. We never dreamed we would work on so many different weapons systems and have such a significant impact. We never dreamed that we would build large teams that would have dozens of partners. If you don't believe me, you can read our original business plan (in the Appendix).

Since those early days, the company's success has skyrocketed. Torch Technologies has more than 1,200 employee-owners and finished 2022 with over $620 million in revenue, making Torch one of the largest federal contractors in the nation. We believe that our level of success is achieved by giving every employee-owner a stake in the outcome.

Torch began with a goal of doing $1 million in business in our first year. Instead, we did almost $3 million. We followed that up with years at $6 million, $9 million, and $15 million, landing us our first spot in the Inc. 5000 list. We would go on to make that list fifteen years in a row. (As best we can tell, only five other companies have accomplished that feat.)

This rate of growth has become contagious, as it seems our growth will continue to accelerate into this year and beyond. What's amazing is that it's easy to overlook the simplicity of our recipe for success, which is based on trusting our employees to act like owners and giving them a voice in planning how and where we want to grow. It really is as simple as that.

Torch has also been the recipient of many local and national awards. We have been recognized by the Better Business Bureau with an ethics award (three times), named Best Place to Work by the Huntsville Chamber of Commerce and *Fortune* magazine multiple times, and were declared one of the best small businesses in the country by *Forbes* magazine. Torch was also named Small Business Prime Contractor of the Year by the United States Small Business Administration. What's really special is that we never sought out these accolades. Rather, they served as validation that we were truly building something special together. (The Appendix covers the full list of awards we have won over the years.)

As we had planned, our success has continued to reward our employees. The first year we gave our employees stock options, a share in the company was valued at seven cents per share. After we formed the employee stock ownership plan (ESOP) and made our first contribution to it in 2004, one share was worth twelve cents. While that seems tiny in retrospect, those numbers have become significant.

Employees who remain at Torch have seen their stock grow

more than 32,000 percent in value. If you invested $1,000 at the end of 2004, it would be worth over $325,000 today. (A similar $1,000 investment in the stock market would have netted you $4,770.88. That's a 377.88 percent return.[1]) For added context, if Torch were a public company, it would have generated a similar compound annual growth rate (CAGR) over the past twenty years as companies like Apple and Netflix—and better than that of Amazon and Nike.[2] That's unbelievable.

Don and I are beyond happy with this success because it is what we always wanted for our employees. It was never about Don and me getting a big check for selling the business. We wanted to build a company that would generate enough wealth for our employees to retire comfortably.

But for us to achieve this financial success at Torch, we also had to deliver value to our customer: the US government. Torch has contributed to the success of many programs throughout the past twenty years.

We have offices located around the world: Huntsville, Alabama (HQ, TIPC, TIPC II); Shalimar, Florida; Albuquerque, New Mexico; Colorado Springs, Colorado; Patuxent River, Maryland; Aberdeen, Maryland; Honolulu, Hawaii (PWC); Detroit, Michigan; and Boston, Massachusetts. Additionally, we have employees at the following locations: Wright Patterson

---

1. S&P 500 Data, "Stock Market Returns Since 2004," no date, https://www .officialdata.org/us/stocks/s-p-500/2004.

2. This context was provided by John Jeffery, Corporate Retirement Director, Financial Wellness Director, CRPS®, QPFC®, and Financial Advisor, First Vice President Morgan Stanley Wealth Management.

Company	20-year CAGR%	Maximum Drawdown During Period
Monster Beverage	41.88%	-66.38%
Apple	38.15%	-56.91%
Netflix	34.75%	-79.90%
Nvidia	31.84%	-79.39%
Intuitive Surgical	28.91%	-72.94%
Old Dominion Freight	27.74%	-42.03%
Illumina	26.70%	-62.98%
Amazon	25.64%	-54.16%
Credit Acceptance	23.42%	-60.85%
ANSYS	22.52%	-57.36%
Tractor Supply	22.28%	-56.23%
IDEXX Laboratories	22.27%	-51.98%
Pool Corp	19.48%	-70.27%
Nike	17.71%	-50.42%
Ross Stores	17.60%	-45.57%
Churchill Downs	16.87%	-43.61%
Johnson Controls	14.70%	-57.41%
NVR	14.68%	-64.52%
Microsoft	14.53%	-54.86%
Altria	14.49%	-40.81%
Microchip Technology	12.81%	-51.41%
JP Morgan	11.42%	-53.26%
Oracle	11.96%	-35.57%
Nestle	11.52%	-34.14%
Disney	10.62%	-54.04%

AFB, Ohio; Fort Sill, Oklahoma; Corpus Christi, Texas; Fort Rucker, Alabama; Langley AFB, Virginia; Washington, DC; Eglin AFB, Florida; Barking Sands, Hawaii (PMRF); Tyndall AFB, Florida; Vandenberg AFB, California; Hanscom AFB, Massachusetts; Kwajalein Atoll (RTS), Marshall Islands; and Cairo, Egypt. We will continue to add locations as the company grows.

Our first military contracts were with the Common Missile Program Office, which later became the Joint Air-to-Ground Missile (JAGM) program. Then we partnered with US Army Aviation and Missile Research, Development and Engineering Center (AMRDEC), supporting the Patriot Missile system. We would go on to further major defense programs, such as Javelin and THAAD Army TACMS, GMLRS, Stinger, HiMARS, SDB, SDB-II, TASM, JASM, Longbow, and many more. Basically, we support virtually all Army, Missile Defense Agency (MDA), and US Air Force missiles and rockets, as well as most aircraft and ground launchers. We have now also built two large laboratories as prototyping and solutions facilities.

We also developed a large subsidiary called Torch Systems that supported the major prime contractors doing systems engineering for large weapon programs. Due to a change in contracting rules in 2009, Torch spun this company off. We then arranged financing so the employees could purchase the company through an ESOP. It was renamed nLogic and went on to be very successful, with ten straight years on the Inc. 5000 list while also earning many outstanding business awards.

Through Torch's success, we created a holding company,

Starfish Holdings, Incorporated. Starfish is the parent company of Torch, and this enables us to create other businesses (such as Freedom Real Estate and Asteroidea) that can be operated totally independently so as not to impact the success of Torch. However, they also offer growth for all our employee-owners through the ESOP, which is now at the Starfish level.

This book is a way to recognize and thank all of the investors, employee-owners, families, and community members who have sacrificed and contributed so much of their time and energy into making Torch Technologies and Starfish Holdings the engines of prosperity they have become. This book could only have been written because of all of you.

I would also be very remiss if I didn't recognize my wife and my two daughters' contributions and sacrifices to my sanity when we were starting up the company. My family tolerated the long hours, the days I returned frustrated, and the many times that I worked so late into the night that they never knew I came home. They tolerated being thrifty, as the income of the entrepreneur can be minimal or inconsistent in the early days of the company. An entrepreneur's family must make sacrifices, sometimes substantial ones, to help them live their dream. I still hurt inside at times for some of their sacrifices. Some opportunities can never be reclaimed.

When we started the company, my pay was minimal for a substantial time. In fact, when I dug through my old files, I saw at what point I was finally able to pay myself a salary of $40,000 a year and raise that much later to $75,000. This was less than a quarter of what I had been making with my former employer when they showed me the door. The truth was that the rapid growth of Torch created cash flow challenges, which meant that many times we couldn't afford to pay me anything. That's why it can be said that the sacrifices an entrepreneur's family is forced to make are extraordinary and endless.

Despite these burdens carried by our families, Don and I somehow found a way to keep the dream alive. We have been so very fortunate. God has blessed us, and we only hope we have appropriately shared those blessings with our employees and community. It's my cherished hope that the next generation is ready to "Keep the Dream Alive," and take Torch into its next evolution.

Now, let's start at the beginning with the story of how Torch came to be. Those who know me well, know I'm an emotional man whose tears come easily. I can admit that reflecting on everything we built together and all the lives we impacted in such positive ways has choked me up more than once. I only hope it tugs on your heartstrings a bit as well.

CHAPTER ONE

The First Day of the Rest of My Life

As the door shut behind me and I left the stale air conditioning behind, the warm and humid Virginia air hit me full in the face. As a bigger guy, it was only a matter of time before I started to sweat. So, I took off my suit coat and loosened my tie before walking to the street corner. That's when I looked down and realized I was still holding the envelope I was given back inside the building. What was in that envelope finally hit me: a check with the biggest number on it I had ever seen. It wasn't quite lottery-winning money, but it was a really nice amount.

As the sun beat down on my head, I started thinking about what that check meant. It was my severance. That check was payment for all the blood, sweat, and tears I had invested in helping my employer, Nichols Research, grow as a business for more than fifteen years. I had expected to finish my career there, earning a gold watch for my long service to the company. But it wasn't Nichols anymore; we had been acquired by Computer Sciences Corporation (CSC) about a year earlier. After that, everything had changed—big time.

From Humble Roots

I started working for Nichols in Huntsville, Alabama, in 1986, as an entry-level scientist. I'd moved to Huntsville from rural Kentucky a year earlier with my wife, Brenda, to take a job with a different company, Dynetics. After graduating with a master's degree from the University of Kentucky, I had considered pursuing my PhD, but the lure of making good money as a scientist was too strong for someone who grew up poor in rural Appalachia.

I enjoyed the work I was doing at Dynetics—reverse engineering foreign military equipment—and I might have continued to work there, until one fateful day when I stopped by the copy room. Someone had left a paper on the copier listing the salary of everyone in my department. I was crushed to realize I was paid the least. So, I decided to apply for something that paid more, which is how I landed at Nichols.

In my first job at Nichols, I worked on solving problems for the US government, specifically doing work on laser radar systems for the branches of the Department of Defense (DoD). Early on, I was able to work on intriguing projects involving rockets and missile guidance systems. I liked the idea that what I was doing was helping to protect our warfighters out in the field.

I also showed an aptitude for leading and managing projects. I received good recommendations from my clients, which helped propel me up the corporate ladder. When I was twenty-eight, I was given the opportunity to help open an office in Utah under the guidance of a senior Nichols employee. But that senior employee decided not to go, so I took on the work. Every office basically operated as an independent company, so I learned a lot on the fly about what it took to run a business.

After a few years there, I accepted another opportunity to move to the Albuquerque, New Mexico, office. That Albuquerque office had been losing a lot of contracts at the time, and they wanted me to help turn things around.

I remember I reached out to a customer to find out why they had canceled our contract. The customer (let's call him Bob) told me they had paid us $50,000 to conduct research and produce an analysis report—the report was never completed.

I immediately apologized and offered to complete the report myself. "Bob," I said, "I believe in the company I work for. And we can make good on the work you paid for."

"Fine," Bob said, "but I want it by tomorrow."

Realizing it was the afternoon already, I knew I had my work cut out for me. The research had been done; all I had to do was compile it into an understandable report. I stayed at the office all night—even forgetting to call Brenda to let her know where I was. (Since this was the pre–cell phone days, she was panicked worrying about me.)

But I completed the analysis report and hand-delivered it to Bob by 8 a.m.

I soon learned why Bob needed the report so fast: He was due to brief his boss a few days later. After he reviewed my work, Bob was excited. "This was the data I was looking for," he told me. He then asked for my help in further refining the report into a presentation he could give to his boss. When he knocked his boss's socks off with the report—getting an "attaboy" as a bonus—Bob renewed his contract with us. Even better, he recommended us to everyone he knew. Before long, the office was bustling with thirty people chasing all the new work we had on our desks.

That was a real lesson in why it's worth going the extra mile for your customers.

Leaping at an Opportunity

After about four years, I was in the position of deputy office manager when I got word from the regional vice president (VP) that my boss was retiring, and I was being promoted to office manager. I was nervous (I was still young to take on the position) but also excited about the opportunity. That's when another executive threw cold water on the deal, saying they wanted to run a wider search to fill the position.

At first, being the good company man, I told them I was okay with that, but I was still interested in taking the position.

When I saw the final short list—without me on it—I realized it was filled with people I had no interest in working either for or with. The culture we had established was very important, and it was not shared by the person selected. So, I decided to turn in my resignation and start my own company. It was a bold move, but I was feeling confident I could make things work.

I got home, and found Brenda upset. "What's wrong, honey?" I said.

Turns out that Chris Horgen, the CEO of Nichols, whom we had met on occasion at regional meetings, had called our home, looking for me. But when Brenda answered the phone, he proceeded to say how tough it was to start your own government contracting business—especially when you had two young kids and a wife to provide for.

"Do you have enough savings to survive for sixty or even ninety days?" he asked Brenda. The short answer was no, we didn't, which was why she was so upset.

While that was a slick a move on Chris's part, he was also showing me he didn't want Nichols to lose me. They offered to move us back to Huntsville with a promotion. We took the deal.

Life Throws Me a Curveball

I made the most of it over the next few years—even earning a promotion to VP. After that, I was one of the youngest executives in the company, and I quickly bonded with the other young guys, such as John Watson. When we all gathered for meetings, John and I would be huddled in a corner catching up about our kids while the other executives bragged about their grandkids.

One day in 1997, Mike Mruz (the president of Nichols) paid me a visit. After closing the door to my office, he told me some big news: I was one of five people he was considering in his succession plan to take over as either president or CEO of the company. But there was a catch. "If you're interested in competing for the promotion," he told me, "you need to move to DC." Nichols was planning to move its headquarters to our nation's capital, and whoever became the next president or CEO needed to be based there.

I had already moved five times across the country for the company, but this one was going to hurt. We had just renovated our house and put in a new swimming pool. We also had a beautiful yard—Brenda's pride and joy. She had won Yard of the Month multiple times from our neighborhood association. But, after talking over the potential promotion with Brenda, we decided to throw my hat in the ring—and off we went to DC.

The next two years were, admittedly, a bit of a blur as I continued to build up my division's portfolio of work, which covered projects for the Army, Air Force, and intelligence agencies. But even in my role as a VP, I didn't understand how the rest of the company was struggling. As a publicly traded company, Wall Street expected us to hit our numbers. And we had for years—until we didn't. It happened again after missing projections for a quarter, and the company's stock took a nosedive.

The predators—already circling—attacked, and it was CSC who came up with the winning bid to acquire Nichols.

Anytime two large companies merge, there are going to be staffing redundancies. That always means layoffs. But even as they started sending some Nichols people home, I got the message that they had a plan for me at CSC.

CSC was organized differently than we were at Nichols. While we structured ourselves around projects, they based themselves around customers. Army contracts went in one division and contracts for the Air Force went in another. Suddenly, most of the people and projects that reported to me were reassigned elsewhere, which left me with a much smaller group to manage. Where once I had about three hundred people reporting to me, now I had a dozen.

Worse, I had made promises to these employees. As a Nichols executive, I could promise them raises, bonuses, and even promotions based on their performance. CSC had stripped that power away from me. I had given these people my word—my word—and now I couldn't deliver on it. I was beside myself because, if anything, I am someone who does what they say they are going to do.

Things went downhill from there. I learned that the guy I was working for was afraid of me. That might sound egotistical, but it was true. He told me himself, "I'm afraid of you, Bill." He wanted me to just sit in my office, work the transition, and trade stocks for two years until he could retire.

Soon, the transition work was minimal, and I didn't have much to do. I couldn't stand that, and I was bored. So, I made an appointment to see his boss. I was upset as I explained what was happening and that I had stock options that were coming due in three months. I demanded to be put back in the game. "Play me or trade me," I insisted.

I got traded.

An Uncertain Future

That's how I found myself standing on that street corner with a severance check in my hand. I didn't even have any of my personal effects from my desk with me. They told me they would send it to me later. They just wanted me to leave. So, I did.

I was out of a job. I hadn't planned on that, and I began to wonder what I was going to tell Brenda.

Little did I realize that walking out the door that day would lead me to start a company that would build on everything I had learned at Nichols—and take it to the next level and beyond.

CHAPTER TWO

Starting Up

A fter leaving my job at Nichols, I wasn't sad as much as I was confused about my future. What was I going to do next with my career?

Fortunately, I landed a job with a different defense contractor called Camber Corporation. The company was headquartered in Huntsville, but I worked out of the DC office. They were a good company and employee-owned—a concept I was instantly intrigued by and impressed with. But I didn't last much more than a year since their specialty was low-tech work, not the kind of research science I enjoyed. I was a fish out of water. Looking back, I feel like I at least made a positive impact in my time there by significantly growing the size of the business I had overseen.

As luck would have it, just when I started contemplating my

next move, I got a phone call from Roy Nichols, the founder of Nichols Research.

Working for My Role Model

Roy was someone I had enormous respect for. Everyone loved him, both inside the company and within the community, because he was an icon. He served on multiple boards and was also well known in the defense industry as a national expert in technology. Boy, did he love his tech. To his credit, he also realized he was much better at technology and didn't have much interest in the business side of the company.

That's why he partnered with Chris Horgen, his younger cofounder, to be chief executive officer (CEO) and help run the business. Chris was phenomenal with the numbers and management. Chris was also the guy who kept promoting me and sending me around the country in my days at Nichols. Together, Roy and Chris complemented each other perfectly, like Batman and Robin.

Roy always had a special place in my heart. In the heyday of Nichols, he was insatiable in researching the latest and greatest tech. And he would recruit employees—known as "Roy's Boys"—to work with him on his pet projects. I worked with Roy on more than a few projects over the years. He was always receptive to my opinions and ideas on whatever he was working on. He was also someone who didn't back down from a fight. It's easy to see now how much I learned from him.

So, when he called, I was thrilled despite everything that

had gone down at Nichols after he and Chris had sold the business.

Roy was calling to offer me a job at the new company he had started called Torch Concepts. I knew the minute he called I was going to take the job. I was so excited I didn't even think to negotiate a salary, perks, or anything.

Roy originally named the business Innoverity. But another company in the space, called Verity, sent a cease-and-desist order. One day, Roy was working at a cabin he had on Torch Lake in Michigan. We were making a list of possible new names for the business when it just clicked. "Let's call it Torch Technologies." Well, someone already owned that website, so Roy settled on Torch Concepts.

A funny aside is that a few years later, when I was ready to start my own company, I reached out to the owner of the Torch Technologies web domain, torchtechnologies.com. Turns out this owner was just camped out, so to speak, on the domain; he owned dozens of sites that all looked exactly the same. So, I sent him an email asking if he would sell the domain to me. He replied, and named his price: $50,000. My eyes just about busted out of my head at that. Once I had calmed down, I sent him my counteroffer: $500. A few minutes later, I got his reply: We had a deal.

A Change in Course

The work we did at Torch Concepts was mostly focused on content management software, which was a great place to be during the dot-com boom. The software Roy's team had developed was capable of categorizing web and document searches in ways we now take for granted. Let's say you wanted to receive information daily about "mercury." You could further specify whether you wanted to receive updates on the Mercury spacecraft, the heavy metal, or even the car. That level of categorization was advanced stuff at the time.

We had successfully raised some capital, something like $4 million to $5 million, which included a sizeable chunk of my own money. I had essentially taken over Chris Horgen's role as Roy's partner. He focused on the tech, while my role was to run the business.

I'll admit that I was a bit frustrated at the time because the tech guys were always fiddling with the software and adding new features, which kept delaying our ability to sell it. We were running on fumes when it came to cash. But we finally secured a few sales and even installed the software for a few customers. Everything looked promising.

Until those planes hit the World Trade Center on 9/11, with a third hitting the Pentagon and a fourth crashing in Pennsylvania. The world changed that day. The stock market sank, the dot-com bubble burst, and raising capital became nearly impossible. That meant that some of us began working on reduced or even no salary. It was easy to recognize that we couldn't continue down that path. We were headed toward bankruptcy, and I didn't think Roy was ready to put much more of his money into the business. I didn't think the company was going to survive.

It was time to think of a new direction. I was ready to venture out on my own.

Back to the Future

The more homework I did in terms of searching for an opportunity to pursue, the more I came back to defense contracting. It was a world I knew well, and I knew I was good at it.

So, I began reaching out to some of my best customers from my time at Nichols, seeing what kinds of needs they had. One customer I reconnected with (let's call him Matt) had just received a big promotion and moved into a new organization in the government. Matt told me how excited he was about the opportunity, but also how he was nervous given the challenges of navigating a new organizational culture.

Light bulbs began popping off in my head. If I had learned anything over my career, it was that change creates opportunity. I figured that if I could find a way to make Matt's life easier in his new role, that would open up other contracting opportunities down the road, serving as the seeds for this new business to grow. There was a runway to scale the business rapidly.

But I also figured I needed a secret weapon to make it happen. I knew I could handle running the business, but I needed someone who knew Matt's new organization inside and out. Someone who could show Matt where all the bodies were buried (so to speak) so he could avoid stepping on them.

That someone turned out to be Don Holder.

Rekindling a Connection

I first met Don when I was a junior engineer at Nichols Research. Don had been a government employee and retired from the government to join Nichols. A talented engineer who was also good at bringing in business, he assigned me some analysis and data research and was a good boss. But when I was transferred and tasked with opening our new Utah office, Don and I didn't see each other again for years.

The bizarre thing was that Don looked a lot like my older brother, James Farmer (whom we nicknamed JF), who was a role model to me until his tragic, untimely death. Their resemblance was uncanny. When my sister met Don years later, she agreed that Don and JF could have been twins. Subconsciously, I think that made me trust and feel comfortable around Don immediately. I continue to love Don as a brother to this day.

When I returned to Huntsville after my aborted attempt to leave and start my own business, Don had been promoted to a vice president. I was a level below him, so we didn't run into each other much apart from company-wide meetings.

As I climbed the corporate ladder and became a VP myself, I began to see Don more until I made the move to DC.

When Nichols was sold, it also had a negative impact on Don—just not in the same way it had affected me. Don was older and closer to retirement age. So, when CSC started cutting back on the benefits package, including the retirement plan that Nichols had in place, he decided to jump ship. He moved on to another contractor in town and took a lot of his team with him—maybe fifty people. Don inspired real loyalty among the people who worked for him.

Making Connections

I thought of Don after having that conversation with my long-time customer Matt. I remembered that Don had once worked in the same position Matt was now in, and many of Don's team had once worked in that same organization.

I knew Matt would see real value in working with a company that he knew was loyal to him—which can be tricky when you're new to an organization. Matt knew me well, and if I could offer him the chance to learn from working with Don and his team, I knew that would add real value.

I also knew Don had skills I didn't, especially when it came to developing new business. And he had a team that would likely follow him.

But to make it all work, I had to convince Don to join my new company.

Pitch Time

I invited Don to join me for breakfast at Rolo's on Airport Road in Huntsville. It's one of those greasy spoons where you can get a plateful of eggs, bacon, and pancakes for just a few bucks. It's wonderful.

As he sipped coffee and I downed Diet Coke, I pitched Don the idea of starting a company together. I explained the situation and how, with his help, we were already perfectly positioned to win our first customer from day one. I even sketched out the business plan for Torch Technologies on a napkin as we spoke.

But Don wasn't buying it. "I'm thinking of retiring," he told me. "I've already filed the paperwork. I don't want to deal with the hassle of starting up a business."

I nodded my head in understanding. So, I changed tactics. I asked him what would happen to his team—his people— when he retired. "Don't you want something better for them than what happened to us?" I asked him. "One thing we share in common is that we both care about the people who worked for us."

I elaborated on the shared pain that resulted from the sale of Nichols and how we couldn't deliver on the promises we had made to our direct reports. I wanted to ensure it wouldn't happen again, either to us or to the people who chose to work with us.

I also reminded Don of all the great things we experienced while working at Nichols. We could copy their business model and their approach to winning contracts, then improve upon it. I shared my vision for the kind of company we could build together. For one, it would be employee-owned right from the start. We would also structure the business in a particular way so that it wouldn't have to be sold or go public to cash us out when we retired, which was what happened with Nichols. I also explained that we wouldn't name the business "Holder" or "Roark Research," or something like that, because we wanted it to outlive us.

While the term didn't yet exist, I explained how I wanted to build an Evergreen company[3]—one that would live on for one hundred years and more. The company would stay true to its values of caring for employees, giving back to our community, and doing our best to keep the warfighters in the field safe.

"What do you say, Don?" I said.

"I'll think about it," he told me.

I shook his hand and thanked him for his time as we said our goodbyes, wondering if I would ever hear from him again.

As it turned out, Don did call me back a few weeks later, in September. He was in his car, driving to Oklahoma to see the University of Alabama football team play the University

---

3. The Tugboat Group – Tugboat Institute, "What is Evergreen?" 2023, https://www.tugboatinstitute.com/what-is-evergreen/.

of Oklahoma Sooners in an away game. (Don remains a huge
Bama football fan to this day.)

When I picked up the phone, I could hear the excitement
in Don's voice. He told me he had made a few calls and talked
about the opportunity. He saw starting the company as a way
to pay back some of the people who had helped him become
successful, but who had also been let down by the sale of
Nichols. He told me he still planned to retire in five years, so
we'd better get started soon. "I'm in," he said. "Let's chart out
the path for this company when I get back. Roll Tide!"

We were on our way. (Side note: Alabama lost that game
37–27.)

Starting Up

The first official day of business after we acquired our license
for Torch Technologies was October 9, 2002. I had invested
$100,000 in the last round of funding at Torch Concepts.
So, I asked for that to be our seed money to get us going. We
were effectively a subsidiary. We started out using their office
space, copiers, and phones. That helped get us going, but
it was one of the worst financial mistakes I ever made. We
were essentially trading something like 20 percent equity in
the company for a small investment, office space, and com-
puters. Buying back that equity later on would prove to be
very expensive. But Roy gave us a runway and good advice to
get the business off the ground that we might not have had
access to otherwise.

Technically, I was a joint employee of both Torch companies for a while. I continued to help Roy with contract management and fundraising on a part-time basis as we went through the transition. We structured it so I would be an employee of Torch Technologies and could invoice Torch Concepts for whatever work I did. Roy and I agreed on a set of different rates based on the work I was doing, which ended up helping us establish a basis for future government contract work.

Don and I had refined our business plan based on what we had done at Nichols. In short, Torch Technologies would be a services company providing paid-by-the-hour engineering talent to oversee the development of weapons systems to keep the warfighters safe on the battlefield. We could bill our customers, and we would keep our rates low to help win contracts. Just as importantly, treating our employees well was a top priority. In fact, we put down our commitment to our employees on paper—

Our Commitment to Our Employees

- Attract and Retain High-Quality Personnel
- Provide Quality Management and Leadership
- Provide Rewarding Opportunities for Career Growth
- Provide a Challenging, Rewarding, and Stable Environment
- Reward Exceptional Service
- Encourage Professional Development

- Maintain an Outstanding Overall
  Compensation Package

- Encourage and Enable Employee Ownership

To that last point, we committed to becoming 100 percent employee-owned within ten years by gradually selling our shares in the business to an employee stock ownership plan (ESOP).

We were also committed to being as flat an organization as we could be. Titles meant little to us in the beginning. I was CEO and Don was president. Maybe a few other folks had titles, but they didn't make sense for a company that started out with fewer than twenty-five employees. We didn't hand out a VP title until we had about 150 employees. I had seen how other defense contractors got bloated quickly by handing out titles. They might have 250 employees, and dozens of them are VPs. I was determined not to be that.

Off to a Hot Start

One thing Don and I didn't do was anticipate how quickly our new company would grow and eat through that initial $100,000 in capital we received from Torch Concepts. If we had started like any normal company, that might have been enough. But by hiring a relatively large team early on, the money went quickly.

We consulted with Chris, and he was right that we also faced the issue of a payment gap where we wouldn't be paid for the work we were doing today until the payment came in some eighty to ninety days later. We needed cash on hand to cover payroll until we had enough contract work where we could count on a steady cash flow.

I decided we needed to do a private placement and raise money from individual investors. But the first few people I reached out to—Roy Nichols and Chris Horgen—both declined. While I understood why Roy might have reservations, I was surprised and hurt that Chris wasn't interested. But he said he wasn't going to invest in defense companies anymore. Interestingly, Chris's son Jay would later play a key role in helping the ESOP buy 100 percent of the company.

I also reached out to Jim Moule, who was president of the Air Force business at Nichols for years. He had taken me under his wing when I had moved out to Utah. When I told him my idea for starting a business with Don based on the Nichols business model, he lit up. "I know you're going to be successful," he told me, ready to invest. He had recently sold $50,000 in stock. "I'm going to write you a check for that amount and put it in the mail," he said. "When you have your capital structure worked out and you need the money, you cash that check."

Jim also told me that because we were going to be successful, we were going to need more money than I was planning for. Over the next few weeks, it quickly became apparent that he was right.

By then, I had created a spreadsheet model that broke down the salary of each employee along with when we expected to get paid for the contracts they were working on. We were profitable, but we had a cash flow problem that would limit how fast we could grow. My initial estimates of our cash flow and how much capital we would need to cover our shortages came to about $250,000 to $330,000. So, that was my target amount to raise from the private placement round.

Our basic sales pitch was that we would be profitable from day one. We had contracts in hand and the employees to do the work—we just needed the cash to pay them. Of course, in our private placement memorandum (PPM), we had to list more reasons for why someone *shouldn't* invest. We needed to caution anyone who was interested that they could lose all their money. Little did we know the sweet deal these investors were actually getting.

Raising Capital

Alongside Jim Moule, many of our investors were friends and acquaintances in and around Huntsville. One was Don's friend who owned an auto dealership in town. Another was an investment broker we both knew. Then there was Jeff Kyser, a colleague from my days at Nichols, whom I was trying to recruit to come work for us. Jeff was a talented software engineer who could make a computer do anything. He was also one of the hardest workers I knew, the kind of guy who was logged on to his computer at midnight to work on a company project. I wanted him on our team, so I invited him to breakfast to give him my pitch.

I quickly learned that Jeff had a high-paying consulting job that he told me he couldn't afford to leave, especially to work for a start-up. "I'm sorry, Bill, but I can't come work with you," he told me, dashing all my hopes. I thought I had wasted my time.

But then Jeff surprised me by asking why I hadn't brought one of our PPMs with me.

"Well, Jeff, I was trying to recruit you to come work for me, not to invest in the business," I said.

That's when Jeff told me that he had inherited some money and that he'd like to invest. Pleasantly surprised, I hustled out to my car to grab a copy of our PPM for Jeff, who invested $30,000 in the business. A few years later, he also joined Torch as an employee.

One potential source of funds we weren't allowed to pursue was the investors in Torch Concepts. The board had told us they were off-limits. But when they heard about it, a few of them were hopping mad—they were ready to mutiny because they wanted in. A couple reviewed it and passed. But three of them immediately took a stake in Torch Technologies as well.

Don and I also made the pitch to a local investment fund where, coincidentally, the former chief financial officer (CFO) of Nichols had gone to work. He knew me and Don well, and he told his colleague Remigus Shatus that we were as good a bet to invest in as anyone. He said, "Don can sell ice to an Eskimo and Bill can find a way to make a profit on it." Without doing any further due diligence, we got a check from that fund for $100,000.

In the end we raised what we needed and more—about $426,000—just forty-eight hours after the private placement memorandum was completed in February. We had to turn away people after that. We were off and running.

Off to the Races

Don and I will be forever grateful to those early investors who put their trust in us and our team. Hopefully, the massive returns they all received in time were worth the effort. In fact, many of them donated a significant portion of all their earnings—millions of dollars in several cases—to nonprofits in the community.

I remember talking to Jim Moule years later when he told me that Torch gave him the best return of any investment he ever made. "I should have sent you more money in the beginning," he told me.

CHAPTER THREE

Up and Running

hen Don and I officially opened the doors to the Torch
offices, we were just getting started. We didn't officially
have any employees or contracts—yet. In fact, the night
before we officially launched, I was putting together some tables
and chairs I had bought for the small office we had rented to
serve as our headquarters in the back of First Commercial Bank.
We were operating on a lean budget right from the start. (I have
been accused more than once of being cheap, but I wanted to be
a good steward of our investors' money.)

Don and I soon found ourselves stepping on each other's
toes in our different roles in leading the business. There was an
inside joke going around in those early years about who was
"Don's guy" or who was "Bill's guy." We decided we had to
agree on how we would divide our duties in a way that would

allow the entire team to focus on building a unified culture and company together.

So, Don and I sat down at our conference table and wrote down the things we thought we could individually do to help lead the business. We each had eight or ten items that we thought we were good at. On my list, I wrote things related to the mechanics of the business, like billing and invoicing, and administering the 401(k) plan and other benefits. Don's list included items related to hiring the right employees to work for us and landing the right customer contracts to work on. The amazing thing was that business development was our only overlapping item because we both had customer relationships. We agreed to compromise on that one. But all the rest led to a clear definition of our roles inside the business. He managed his list, and I managed mine. It worked well.

I have no doubt that had Don started a business on his own, he would have been successful. I feel the same about myself. But together, we made one incredible leader. We thought very differently, and yet, we complemented each other perfectly. In many ways, we were very similar to Roy Nichols and Chris Horgen in that we were stronger leaders by working together.

A Call to Arms

Early on, Don and I both went to work recruiting people we knew either from our Nichols days or from working with customers at the US Army's Redstone Arsenal. We had a different story to pitch than anyone had heard before. We wanted to take the best of Nichols's great culture and elevate it by making everyone an owner in the business. One thing we stressed early, though, was that we only recruited people who had already left Nichols (which was owned by CSC at that point). We didn't want to anger anyone at CSC—especially any former colleagues we were still friendly with.

Looking back, it's remarkable how spectacular our early recruits truly were. We found folks who had knowledge and relationships in the business that put us in an incredible position to not just write proposals, but also win them and perform. Just as importantly, they were the right people to form a lasting culture of success and caring.

One of my first calls was to Terry Thomas, who had worked for me at Nichols. Terry had jumped ship soon after the CSC acquisition, and we stayed in touch as he bounced around a few other places. I invited him to lunch at a local joint called Cheeburger Cheeburger, where I mapped out the business plan for Torch on a napkin as part of my recruiting pitch. I knew Terry had suffered because of the Nichols sale—like Don and I had—so I explained how we were going to use employee ownership to make sure something like that never happened at Torch.

"Bill, this is a no-brainer," Terry said. "This makes total sense."

I then got to work putting together an official offer letter for Terry. But I learned later on that Terry was getting cold feet about joining Torch.

"I had gone home and told my wife, 'Honey, this is a start-up,'" Terry told me. "I don't have a contract, benefits, or anything. Then my wife said, 'Isn't this what you always wanted to do? You will forever regret not doing this. Stop flirting and go get it done.'"[4]

So, Terry accepted our offer and became employee number six. He was preceded only by me, Don, Dana Renfro, our office administrator, Jaye Bass, and Tina Corley.

In January 2003, Jaye and I landed Torch's first contract for a software consulting project, and I remember Terry and me talking about what opportunities we could chase to help get the company up and running. "Let's go find something to do," I told him. That became somewhat of a mantra I would repeat over the years: Let's create our own opportunities.

As a new business, we had the challenge of building our reputation with potential government customers. Since we were not yet one of the big contractors (known as "primes"), we needed to hunt for projects we could help with by offering our own expertise. If we built relationships with the customers and found out their concerns, we could ask the prime to bring us on as a subcontractor. The primes then typically would charge a fee on the work we promised to do, which would give them an incentive to funnel more work our way.

I was humbled when people like Jaye and Terry agreed to join our team because they were bringing their own reputations and personal networks with them. For someone like Terry, he might have been working with a customer for years on a particular project. If Terry let the customer know he was

---

4. Terry Thomas, in conversation with the author, August 31, 2022.

now working for Torch, the customer would value Terry's experience and expertise to the extent that they would find a way to get Torch a contract for Terry's services.

In a few cases, though, a prime might move to block us from getting a contract. That was a line we pledged never to cross ourselves. And, in fact, it often backfired with the customer anytime someone tried to pull such a stunt. We were building our business on long-term relationships, not short-term transactions. We were also fortunate because the customers we targeted on the Arsenal wanted to help small businesses, especially those based in Huntsville.

Another of my early calls was to Tina Corley, whom I knew well and had a great deal of respect for from our time together at Nichols. Tina left Nichols after the sale to CSC to join the venture capital (VC) fund Chris Horgen started that eventually became Eastside Partners (which would play a key role in Torch's story). As we were just getting started, I knew she could add significant value without having to commit herself full time at Torch.

Tina signed on as a member of our board of directors, our part-time CFO, and Torch's fifth employee. She understood our business development strategy and was extremely helpful in setting our billing rates early on so we could bid competitively for our first contracts. She also set up our retirement plans, employee benefits, insurance policies, financial infrastructure, and compliance programs. Put simply: We couldn't have done it without her.

Just as importantly, as I still like to tell Tina, she kept me from having to wear an orange jumpsuit by ensuring that we never violated any government rules. Tina retired from the Starfish board while I was writing this book. I wrote her a note where I tried (and probably failed) to summarize how important she was to the Torch and Starfish stories. Here's a sample:

> Twenty years ago, I started a journey. It had challenges I didn't understand or appreciate. Some were beyond what I could have accomplished. Fortunately, I had you as a friend to fill in many of those blank spaces. You stepped in and stepped up and made sure that I was doing things the right way. When I strayed, you challenged me and corrected me back to where I should be . . .
>
> You made a difference—thank you for the amazing job you have done. Thank you for your hard work and dedication. I am sad to see you go. I cannot let you leave without wishing you the very best. May your next chapter be fulfilling and filled with happiness. May your cup run over.

It's truly remarkable that we were able to attract people of the highest caliber, like Tina. The story of Torch is as much about them as it ever was about Don and me.

INFORMALITY RULES

I remember back when I worked at Nichols, and Chris Horgen wanted me to move across the country. He invited me into his office, where he had a sofa and armchairs as well as a desk. But when I came in, Chris didn't just sit behind that big old desk. He welcomed me and gave me a seat on his comfortable couch while he took a seat in one of the chairs, which were at something like a sixty-degree angle to the sofa. That created a much more informal and comfortable environment to talk in. There wasn't an invisible barrier or barricade separating us. That made an imprint on me and was the kind of leadership style I wanted to embrace.

You might also have picked up on the fact that I made a lot of deals on napkins. (Tim Thornton, president of Torch Systems [nLogic] was a Torch employee I recruited and hired using a napkin.) That's because I often held meetings at restaurants to take the formality out of a situation. It helps make the conversation more cordial. Most people won't get too riled up in a public restaurant, either. They're going to be civil even if they're upset.

I also preferred having these meetings at breakfast or maybe lunch. That's why my favorite meeting spots included Rolo's, the Blue Plate Diner, and Gibson's, a barbeque joint where I've done a gazillion deals. I also had a lot of meetings at Cracker Barrel. All these places were as informal as you could get.

People will give you real answers to hard questions when you ask them in a non-threatening environment. It's tough to get uptight when you're having eggs and toast or biscuits and gravy. That's why I never took anyone to a fancy restaurant like Cotton Row to talk business. We'd only go there if we had something to celebrate.

Later on, when the company got bigger, it became a popular thing for me to take a dozen employees out to

continued

lunch without their supervisor. It gave them the opportunity to talk about whatever they wanted, and I got a lot out
of those conversations. We changed policies and added
benefits like bereavement leave based on those informal
conversations. It was also a great forum to answer people's
questions about the ESOP and employee ownership.

When we started having our executive off-site meetings, I used to make time to meet with each person's
spouse and give them the chance to ask anything they
wanted—and good Lord, did they. I remember getting
grilled one time by the wife of an executive who wanted to
know why I kept her husband working until 9 p.m. every
night. I explained that we didn't make him stay. "He chose
to stay late because he was trying to change your life by
advancing his career and growing the value of the ESOP,"
I told her.

We once even sent the spouses for a day, in a limo,
from the off-site in Nashville to visit the Jack Daniels dis-
tillery in Lynchburg, Tennessee. They had a blast. That
kind of thing went a long way in terms of building loyalty
among the families of our employees who were sacrificing
a lot early on to help build our company.

Getting the Band Back Together

As I was reaching out to folks I knew we wanted to recruit, Don
was working on his own recruiting pitch to the team of talented engineers who had followed him from Nichols to CAS,
another defense contractor. CAS had run into some trouble
due to a hiccup with the government. That was unpopular

to say the least, especially with people like Don. That's why he was planning to retire until I convinced him to join me in starting Torch. It turned out that the changes helped convince other people who reported to Don and were planning to move over to Torch as well.

Joe Hill, Don's right-hand man, came first (earning him designation as employee number seven—or double-oh-seven). He was followed by others like Joe Robinson, Clayton Newkirk, and Joe Hill's long-time friend Janet Haenisch, all of whom had worked for Don for years. They also happened to be working together on a critical missile project for the US Army that we hoped to bring over to Torch.

"It was like keeping the band together," said Janet, who didn't know me well before coming in for her interview with me and Don. "We were a pack of wolves that stayed together. I admit I am not easy to convince, and I was skeptical. But Joe was telling me that this was going to be something special. It also helped that Roy Nichols was involved at the beginning. And after you laid out the concept of employee ownership and how we would have the long-term potential to grow wealth for everyone in the company, I got excited."[5]

Janet and her team all joined Torch on the same day. Frankly, the company was taking on a great deal of risk by hiring people of Janet and her colleagues' caliber. We simply didn't have sufficient money in the bank at that time to cover their salaries for more than a few months. It's still hard to believe we had

---

5. Janet Haenisch, in conversation with the author, September 16, 2022.

the guts to do that and that these folks were willing to take the chance. We were all betting they would be able to help us win the kinds of contracts we could build the business on. And that's exactly what they did.

Joe, Janet, and their team paved the way for Torch to earn its first contract with the Army in early 2003. The country was about to go to war, and we could now offer a customer an entire modeling and simulation team for a defense missile system that was about to be put to the test on the battlefield—and prove itself an invaluable ally for US warfighters.

Our goal for our first year was to earn $1 million in revenue. We ended up at $3 million—and things scaled up quickly after that, even as we overcame some early struggles.

LEARNING AN EARLY LIFE LESSON

I met Clay Hagan back in 1986, when we both worked for Nichols. (Clay was one of my early recruits to Torch.) We had heard about a new golf league that was starting inside Nichols and, coincidentally, both headed to the driving range to dust off our clubs. As we hit balls side by side (often pretty badly), we struck up a conversation. We decided that even though neither of us was a top golfer, we should join the league to meet people. We agreed to team up and play together.

It turned out we had a few other mutual friends join the league with us. But Clay and I were the worst golfers in the group. Just terrible. Our colleagues would constantly give us advice on how to play better, like "tee the ball higher." At one point after buying the tallest tees made, I swung hard, removing the tee so cleanly that the ball dropped to the ground without moving forward even one inch.

Clay and I slowly but surely got better each week. We even started to win our matches—mostly because we had such high handicaps, which evened the odds when we competed against stronger players. In fact, believe it or not, by the final week of the season, Clay and I were in first place! Even better, the team right behind us didn't show up for our final match, which made us the champs. At least, it would have made us champs if we had been older and wiser.

But the second-place team's opponents didn't show up for their final match either. They were older than Clay and me—and better golfers. They were also better at trash-talking, because they goaded us by saying, "It doesn't feel right not to settle this on the field. We're here, so let's play for it." In other words, they wanted us to play them for the championship.

Now, Clay and I have technical degrees, so we did a quick calculation. We decided we were far enough ahead of these guys that we could still win even if we didn't play our best. All we had to do was win four out of the nine holes.

That was easier said than done.

Once we reached the last hole, the other team had won five holes and we had won three holes. We still had a chance to win. It all came down to me. If I made a final short putt of several feet, we would win.

The ball hit the cup and rolled out. I missed. We lost.

I'm not sure Clay ever really forgave me for missing that putt. We ended up in second place and got a plaque for our efforts—something I hung in my office for years where I could see it every day.

continued

> Decades later, Clay was leaving my office, and he noticed the plaque. "Bill, why in the world would you hang that plaque up there?" Clay asked me.
>
> "It's a lesson I want to remember," I told Clay. "That when you have won something, know when to quit."

On Our Own

Early on, we had formed a board of directors to help steer the future direction of the company. It had three members: Don, Roy Nichols, and me. But after our first year, Torch Technologies and Torch Concepts were heading in different directions. Torch Concepts was losing money, and Roy began making an argument in our board meetings that our company should be paying money to them, our holding company. Roy had every right to ask us to do this. But we were also cash-starved in that we needed every penny we had to keep fueling our growth. That's why Roy's request didn't sit well with Don or with me. It was Don who challenged Roy, telling him he had a conflict of interest and couldn't be a board member of both entities. I remember looking at Roy's face. He was stunned. He said something like, "If that's how you feel, then I'll resign." And he did. He got up and walked out, never to return.

In many ways, that was the moment when Torch Technologies had to stand on its own as a company.

The Recruiting Game

When it came to building up the Torch team, every employee played a key recruiting role. For instance, Janet was so excited about the potential at Torch that she started making a list of everyone she could think of who would fit the culture of our new company. This included one of her high school classmates and her husband, Steve Haenisch. In fact, almost all of our first wave of employees came from referrals, and only about 30 percent of them were former Nichols employees.

"The culture became a differentiator and people wanted to come work for Torch," Janet said. "At other companies, the culture was about backstabbing and undercutting others and being unfair to subcontractors. Yet, I had multiple people say to me, 'I never heard anything bad about Torch.' We were doing things differently. We also knew that when [this] kind of talent joined us at Torch, their work would likely soon follow them."

When people like Steve joined the team, they brought talent in areas that helped expand the business. At one point, we probably had thirty-five people working in thirty different areas.

"Bill and Don built a team that brought many different backgrounds both in terms of their skills and their personal contacts with customers," Joe Hill said. "Because of that, we had an incredible diversity of customers early on."[6]

For example, Steve had been working for the Missile

6. Joe Hill, in conversation with the author, September 29, 2022.

Defense Agency in the US Department of Defense (DoD) for years. It was just a matter of the customer learning more about who we were at Torch before they wanted to work with us, as well. "When a company is good to its employees, that's also good for the government," Steve said. "It's to their advantage that an employee is happy and well cared for."[7]

At the same time, Steve knew he and Janet were taking a big risk as a married couple working for the same company. "But I also knew about Don and Bill's reputations as ethical and honest people," Steve said. "Bill made it clear they were building an employee-owned company from the get-go, and it was exciting to get in on the ground floor of something that could be special." Steve also knew that if Torch imploded, he was valuable enough to his customer that he could most likely transfer to another contractor to continue working on his project. Put another way, even though we were asking people like Steve and Janet to join a start-up, they could see far more upside than potential downside in making the move. They were super smart engineers, after all. Nearly twenty years later, it seems clear that Steve and Janet—now both retired from Torch—made the right move.

But not everyone we were reaching out to was ready to make the leap to join the Torch team. For some, it remained too much of a risk. It was essentially a chicken-and-egg scenario. We needed to grow to become a more stable business, but we couldn't grow unless we had the people and the contracts. In

---

7. Steve Haenisch, in conversation with the author, September 13, 2022.

those first few years, that meant all of the early employees were doing everything they could to not just earn new business with our customers, but also to lay the foundation for our company to grow into the future.

I also have always believed I cannot ask anyone to do something I am not willing to do myself. So, in those early days, I did everything I could—from taking out the trash to running finances and troubleshooting information technology (IT) problems—to get our business up and running. And I wasn't alone. We all did what was needed to be successful. "We were all secretaries, we were all security people; everybody had to wear five hats," said Terry.

Janet Haenisch, for example, took on the task of writing our first employee handbook, despite the fact she didn't have experience in human resources (HR). "I did research from other employee handbooks of companies who had good benefits, and I picked what I thought best," said Janet. "We all pitched in and did whatever needed to be done."

What was also remarkable about those first few years was that most Torch employees—including Don and me—spent much of their time with our customers on-site. People like Joe, Janet, Terry, and Clayton would work forty hours on their projects, and then head over to the Torch offices to tackle Torch-specific tasks, like holding strategic planning and business development meetings and applying for contracts. We were attempting to build a company culture with a group of employees who essentially worked remotely. Perhaps unlike most other businesses, we were asking our people to work

nights and weekends on the business on top of what the customer was paying them to do. We simply didn't have the
overhead to hire full-time people to cover all the work that
needed to be done. It was a big ask.

That wasn't ideal when it came to building our business,
but we all found a way to manage it. And a big reason why was
because everyone had a true stake in the outcome as an owner
in the business. "Unlike in other companies I had been at, I
knew I wasn't working to make someone else wealthy," Janet
said. "I was betting on the potential we shared as owners."

When we'd meet for morning meetings at 7 a.m., I would
bring in McDonald's sausage biscuits by the bagful to give
everyone something to eat while we talked. I thought it was
great because they were only ninety-nine cents each. But,
after a while, someone complained and asked if we could
have something better—maybe something from Hardee's.
Well, that was a big leap for me to make, as those cost $1.99
each. But I relented and even threw in some chicken biscuits
now and then. Once they came to town, we even upgraded
to Chick-fil-A sandwiches. When you add all those calories
together with all the candy we used to keep on hand—including bags of M&Ms, Kit Kats, and Three Musketeers—some
of us noticed we had started to gain weight. Soon, we were
calling the extra pounds we were adding on the "Torch Ten."
But attending those Torch meetings after hours and on weekends also required some personal sacrifices from our early team
beyond their waist sizes.

Case in point: Clayton Newkirk, employee number sixteen,

joined the team in February 2003. At that point, he had spent more than a decade working with his customers on-site at the Arsenal. With a wife and two young kids at home, he admitted it was difficult at times to find the right work-life balance in those early years. One time, Clayton came up to me and mentioned how one of his son's T-ball games conflicted with a Torch meeting. To me, the priority was clear. "The T-ball game is more important," I told him. "Go." To me, that was a chance to prove that we were putting our people and their families first, even as we asked so much of them in helping to build up the business.

"Bill made it clear from the first day that our bonus would depend on how well Torch did," Clayton said. "He wanted to shed that internal competition even as he pushed us to grow into uncomfortable new areas."[8]

When we began holding regular meetings on Thursdays in our Torch offices, that also created some friction with some of our customers. It required our team to perform a delicate tap dance to prove they were performing at a high level for the customer in a way that earned them the right to sneak out to attend a meeting.

"They were definitely not happy when we weren't there," Clayton said about telling a customer that he was leaving for the day. "I was constantly worried about how if I did too much for Torch, I would jeopardize our work at the Arsenal. But Bill

---

8. Clayton Newkirk, in conversation with the author, September 14, 2022.

and Don always made it very clear that if a customer cut us off tomorrow, Torch would be there to take care of us."

In It Together

The tenet of our culture to put our people first was put to the test at the end of our second year in business. We were on a roll, winning just about every subcontract proposal we bid on. Right around Christmastime, we lost a bid for a contract we had been working for the US Army Space and Missile Defense Command. At the time, we had grown to about sixty people, and losing this subcontract impacted about ten of our employees. It was a devastating blow.

I distinctly recall where I was when we got the news about that particular subcontract. I was on vacation in Orlando, Florida, and I was standing in a golf shop in an outlet mall. I called back to Huntsville and told someone to call a meeting with the employees impacted by that subcontract and tell them not to take a job with anyone else until I returned. (I decided not to buy the set of clubs I was considering.)

When I got back, Don and I gathered everyone together to share the bad news. You could feel the tension in the air. Everyone in the defense contracting business knows that once you lose a contract, the next thing to follow is layoffs. But we weren't going to do that at Torch.

"We're not laying anyone off," we said. "Nobody is going home. The client did what they thought was best, but we'll find a way through this."

I got together with the ten employees impacted—nine engineers and an administrative employee. I made it very clear to all of them that we didn't want to lose anyone. "We are a growing company now, and we can afford to keep paying your salaries," I told them. "We will find other work and projects for you. We don't want to see you go."

After we ended the meeting, the team's admin came up to me and asked if she was really able to keep her job. "I am an admin and not an engineer," she said. "I wanted to make sure I heard you correctly that I can keep my job."

"Of course you can keep your job," I told her. "You're just as much a part of Torch as any engineer." Which was the truth: Our admins play a critical role in building and maintaining our relationships with our customers.

Well, you know what she did? She broke down in tears. This kind of thing just wasn't done in our industry at the time. But none of our people left. It was clear to everyone inside the company that we valued everyone—from engineers to admins—and that we were committed to everyone who was an owner in our company.

That was a turning point for our young company. From that moment on, everyone knew we were truly in it together.

History seems to have a way of repeating itself. In late November of 2013, we lost the recompete of our first major prime contract. This prime contract had generated 25 percent of our revenue that year. Like we had done in 2004, I gathered the impacted employees and told them we wanted to keep them all. A few of the subcontractors we worked with on that contract heard what we had done, and they decided to follow our lead. They kept their employees as well, rather than letting them go.

We have always prided ourselves on doing the right thing, even with our subcontractors. I like to think of it as acting like a "benevolent prime" (though I have to admit that not everyone loves that phrase). We were paving a way for a new approach to building a culture that truly valued our fellow employees as family. I am so proud of those employees who decided to stay with us. I may be even happier that several of them have since retired comfortably because of the ESOP—which is a fulfillment of the vision Don and I had when we started Torch.

A nice wrinkle to the ending of this story is that a few months after we lost the bid, we got a call from the winning company. Because they had been so unsuccessful in recruiting to their team any of our people who had been working for the customer, they offered to bring us on as a subcontractor. We gave this some thought and ultimately agreed to the deal.

CHAPTER FOUR

Ownership for All

As great of a culture as we had back at Nichols Research, ownership was held by only a few individuals, such as the founders. When they started Nichols, they had also given a percentage of ownership to another early employee.

But, when that person died many years later, Roy and Chris didn't have the cash on hand to pay his estate for his share of the business. That's when Roy and Chris decided to take Nichols public to raise some cash while also cashing out some of their equity. Of course, going public had a big impact on the culture of the company—eventually setting it up to be acquired by CSC.

The thing that bothered me the most was that Roy and Chris were essentially forced to sell the business by going public as a way for them to cash out their interests. When Don and

I started Torch, we wanted to build a different escape hatch for when it came time for us to leave the business. We didn't want to have to sell the company if one of us decided to leave the business. After all, Don was nearing retirement.

Don and I both were committed to the notion that we wanted our company to be 100 percent employee-owned within ten years. But we didn't really know how it would work out at first. Did that mean that 100 percent of employees would own stock in the business? Or was there another model we could explore?

One of the options I learned about was the employee stock ownership plan (ESOP). I had experienced what it was like to be part of an ESOP during the year I worked for Camber before leaving to work with Roy Nichols at Torch Concepts. I really liked the idea of it. Another major contractor in Huntsville, Dynetics, was also an ESOP at the time. ESOPs force companies to conduct an annual valuation, which sets the stock price. Employee-owners can then see what the new valuation means to their accounts—all of which they can pull up with the click of a computer mouse.

If, like me, you attend employee ownership conferences, you also realize that ESOPs can mean different things to different people. For Torch, we saw it as a retirement mechanism that augmented our 401(k) program. It also bonded our employees together to work for a common goal they would all benefit from attaining. Just as importantly, the ESOP also provides the mechanism to buy the founder out when they leave, so you don't have to sell the company or go public.

There was also a strong case that the ESOP fit our business model to a T. It's a natural fit for a services contractor doing business with the DoD because you can make the ESOP contribution part of the benefits package. That way, it becomes a billable part of your overhead rates, just like health care, 401(k), or life insurance. At the same time, we knew our government customers liked the stability that would come from working with a company owned by its employees. Since our employees would own the company, they could also better control costs and bid on contracts more effectively than our competitors. Why? Because they had a true stake in the outcome when we were successful. If we keep our costs down and perform as owners, our customers benefit, and thus, we all benefit.

The topic of employee ownership is a central one to the Torch story. It's woven into our company's DNA. Just about every story I share in these pages is impacted in one way or another by our decision to share broad-based ownership within our business right from the start—day one.

A Stake in the Outcome

Around the same time I began researching the topic of ESOPs in earnest, I came across a book written by Jack Stack, the president and CEO of SRC Holdings in Springfield, Missouri. Jack had spun off a failing factory from International Harvester Company in 1983, to save the jobs of its one hundred employees—a journey he also wrote

about in *The Great Game of Business*, his first book. But in
the process of trying to borrow the money he needed to buy
the factory, Jack recognized that he had been taught how to
make great products—they remanufactured big truck and
farm tractor engines—but no one had ever taught him or his
team how to build a company.

In that moment of clarity, Jack recognized that he couldn't
rebuild their company alone. He needed everyone inside the
business to do that. That's when he seized on the concept that
he could demystify business for his employees by getting them
to understand that it wasn't any more complicated than learning to play a game like Monopoly. By teaching them the rules,
creating a scoreboard, and sharing a stake in the outcome, he
could build a business of businesspeople.

In *A Stake in the Outcome*, his second book, Jack mapped
out the journey that SRC went through as it became employee-
owned through its ESOP. It was the phrase "stake in the
outcome" that really thrilled me. In some ways, I was jeal-
ous that I hadn't coined it myself, because it almost perfectly
encapsulated what we wanted to create at Torch.

The more we learned about ESOPs like the one Jack and
SRC adopted, the more we thought it would also be the perfect model with which to build Torch's culture. Not only was
it a retirement plan for the employees where their stake would
grow as the value of the business grew, but it also offered a
way for the founders to sell their equity in the business to the
ESOP—keeping the company owned by the employees. We
knew right from the start, for example, that Don was planning

to retire in five or six years. That meant we needed to prepare from our first day in business to cash Don out in a way that wouldn't force us to sell the company. We didn't want to have anyone repeat our experience at Nichols.

We wanted everyone to share in the rewards of building up the value of the business. That was our commitment to everyone who joined our team because we wanted our employees to do well financially. As long as we were growing the value of the business, they would share in that success. I wanted everyone to be able to retire comfortably. One could argue there is a socialist component to this model because everyone in the company does well. I really like the idea that nobody is left behind. And, when everyone has a stake in the outcome, they're truly motivated to go above and beyond in making the company successful.

There is a capitalist component as well. We can motivate those who make a difference in the company with additional ownership outside the ESOP. We did that initially by issuing stock options. Once we became 100 percent employee-owned, we switched to using synthetic stock appreciation rights (SARs). I often say we have the best of both philosophies. It is the employee's choice on what they achieve.

Our folks pull together and work for each other more than people have done at any one place where I have worked. Other companies are envious of us because everyone puts their shoulder to the wheel. We would not have been as successful as a company if we hadn't found a way for all of us to work together as well as we have.

The Core of Ownership

Building the foundation for Torch Technologies on a core of employee ownership also became a significant recruitment tool for us, especially in the early days. Since we were cash-poor in the beginning, we couldn't offer exorbitant salaries to the talented people we wanted to join our team. In fact, many of the earliest Torch management employees agreed to take pay cuts of 20 percent to 30 percent. Why would anyone do that? It was because they saw the potential of joining a business on the ground floor as an owner. Admittedly, not everyone understood the concept right away. Employee ownership was still a relatively novel concept at the time. But, when we did get the chance to explain it, you could see people's eyes light up.

Case in point: When we got the opportunity in 2004 to recruit Brady Porter, a young engineer who had worked for both Don Holder and Steve Haenisch, he didn't know much about what employee ownership meant. Prior to Torch, Brady's job had required him to work a lot of hours—including weekends, which required sacrifices. He was newly married and had a young child. That meant he was spending a lot of time away from his young family. And for what? "I remember thinking that something wasn't right," Brady said. "I was breaking my neck to make this project successful. But it wasn't clear how that work and sacrifice would help my career."[9]

After we successfully recruited Brady to join our team, he saw the power of the ESOP in action. He saw how his hard

---

9. Brady Porter, in conversation with the author, November 14, 2022.

work would not only help build the value of the business but would also benefit him and his family over the long run by building wealth in the ESOP. "You begin to realize you're not just working for yourself, you're building a future for your family as well," Brady said. "You don't get that at other companies."

Brady, who now runs our advanced engineering concepts group, said he's since used those same lessons to help recruit other talented engineers to Torch. "There's a saying that the grass is always greener where you water it," he said. "Anyone who comes to Torch has a huge opportunity to grow their career while also building wealth through the ESOP over the long term. Just as importantly, you'll find a true family atmosphere at Torch."

Brady is right to point out that sharing ownership not only creates a feeling of family but also helps us avoid the internal competition and infighting we see in some of our larger competitors. A benefit of the ESOP, at the management level especially, was that it created an incentive for employees to cooperate—to focus on building the value of the business instead of building a silo around their area of work.

Sharing Ownership

One catch with ESOPs is that they can be expensive to implement and maintain. There are lots of rules you need to understand so you don't get into trouble. You also need to invest in new practices like getting an outside valuation of the business once a year to establish the value of each participant's stake in the ESOP. For most companies, it doesn't make sense to go down that path until you reach a certain size. Because of these constraints, we agreed that we needed to wait until we had grown the company to at least fifty employees before putting the ESOP in place. Until then, we would offer stock options in Torch to our early wave of employees. In time, the ESOP would then purchase those options.

As it turned out, it took us a little more than a year to reach the fifty-employee mark. We put the ESOP in place in early 2005, retroactive to 2004. The first ESOP shares were worth a whopping twelve cents each. That was the start of putting our ten-year vision in place for Torch to become entirely employee-owned. But to get there, we went through multiple transactions to cash out our various early investors who helped us get up and running.

Our first major transaction on the path to becoming employee-owned came in 2006, when it became clear that Torch Concepts was going to shut down. There was a question at the time about whether the investors in Torch Concepts wanted to purchase the stock in our company (that Torch Concepts held) or whether they'd prefer for us to buy those shares out. After some negotiation, we collectively decided to buy the shares ourselves for the ESOP. But we also needed a financial partner to help us raise the money we needed.

That led us to Eastside Partners, a VC firm headed up by Jay Horgen (Chris's son) and Emerson Fann. We cut a deal with them. They would buy the shares held by Torch Concepts, and we would then repurchase those shares over a five-year period.

That gave us some cash flow cushion to work with while also establishing a clear path for the ESOP to acquire those shares.

The next major transaction came in 2009. Along the way, the ESOP had cashed out a few of our other initial investors as they sought to take some money off the table. Then, we completed our transaction with Eastside Partners by purchasing the remaining shares they held in Torch. That turned out to be a huge growth period for us; we grew to about $30 million in revenue, which boosted the value of the company's stock significantly. Eastside did well on the deal: The stock had risen to offer a seven-time return on the initial investment. Eventually, Eastside Partners agreed to exit Torch Technologies stock in order to structure a very similar deal with Torch Systems (soon to be called nLogic) as part of the spinout.

Now, the ESOP held more than 34 percent of the company's ownership. But in the next two years, we went further. We convinced all our early investors that it was time for them to sell their shares back to us. It was time for Torch to become a 100 percent employee-owned company.

While most of those early investors were willing to cash out (they had all earned an incredible return on their investment), I had to work hard to convince a few of them to sell. But it wasn't about the money. Apparently, owning a piece of Torch stock had become something of a status symbol around town—a kind of club where people could brag that they had gotten in at the beginning of something big. Eventually, I was able to win them over.

Realizing a Vision

There were a lot of emotions attached to buying out our investors and making Torch a truly employee-owned company. There was the excitement of fulfilling the dream Don and I had from the very start. But there were also some nerves. To complete the transaction, we needed to borrow $24 million from some of the selling shareholders and the bank. That was a significant amount of debt to take on at that time in the company's history.

But we also saw an opportunity to offer our employees an even greater stake in the company. As a one-time offer, they could roll over any 401(k) money into the ESOP—which would then be used to buy out the investors. When we talked to bankers about structuring the deal this way, they told us we could expect that our employees might roll over something between $3 million and $6 million. It was voluntary, and we cautioned everyone about having too many eggs in one basket when it came to their retirement investments.

When we tallied the results, our employees had rolled over $12 million, crushing the estimates. We had employees who had only been with Torch for six months or less participate. That meant Torch only needed to borrow something like $12 million, a much more digestible number, to finance the rest of the transaction.

December 2011 was a big moment in Torch's history. We were fully employee-owned but also $12 million in debt! In the end, we paid off our note to the bank within two years. We could have paid it off sooner, but the government was experiencing a shutdown at the time, so to protect our employees' income, we held on to our cash to cover our payroll until customers could start paying again. By 2014, after we paid back the bank debt, Torch was 100 percent owned by its ESOP and 100 percent debt-free. We even had jackets made to celebrate the big day.

A Path to Retirement

The most gratifying thing about the path we chose is seeing how that first generation of Torch employees has been able to retire comfortably, thanks to the success of the company. They are retiring to beach houses or traveling across the country in RVs, living dreams they never thought possible when we started the business twenty years prior. In some cases, their shares in the ESOP might also be giving them the freedom to care for ailing family members, volunteer for charities, or do missionary work.

Whatever they choose to do, it's extremely gratifying for me to see them retire early when they still have good health. We've even changed the rules to allow our employee-owners to retire as early as age sixty if they want, rather than at sixty-five. We are seeing the fruits of all our labors bear out—which is exactly what Don and I had scratched out on that napkin in Rolo's back in 2002.

The mission of employee ownership never ends. It's not a "set it and forget it" kind of system. You must constantly invest in and nurture it. It can be a challenge, for example, to convince new employees—especially members of the younger generations—that their ESOP balance is something worth sticking around for. It's been our experience that it takes around three to five years before someone really begins to understand the kind of impact the ESOP can have on their net worth, especially when combined with their 401(k). In a world where pensions and lifetime employment have faded away, the ESOP remains a true engine for creating wealth for workers.

What's remarkable is that I have personally done better financially based on the growth of my shares in the ESOP than I did when I sold my initial equity to the company.

Planning for the Future

But there's another trap that companies owned by their ESOP face: funding the repurchase liability. In other words, the ESOP must ensure it has enough cash on hand to pay its shareholders, should they decide to cash out. It's a bit of a double-edged sword because as the company grows and increases in value as a result of the efforts of the employee-owners, the cash needed to cover their shares in the ESOP grows exponentially as well. We're talking hundreds of millions of dollars in the case of Torch.

The good news is that ESOP companies are uniquely positioned to plan for their future. ESOP companies that are employee-owned and organized as an S-Corp don't pay income tax (shareholders pay tax individually when they cash out their shares of the ESOP, much like 401(k) distributions). This gives

ESOP companies a healthy edge in generating cash flow that is very much needed to cover their repurchase liability when shareholders retire.

But we've seen multiple examples where companies use their extra cash to make acquisitions or other investments in their growth—leaving them exposed. This is exactly what has happened to many very successful ESOP companies. They are forced to sell to other companies because they couldn't cover the cost of the accounts for their retiring employee-owners. Even one of the groundbreakers of the employee ownership movement, Science Applications International Corporation (SAIC), eventually went public to cover their liability.

So, for Torch to keep true to the mission Don and I had put down on the napkin, we always need to be looking to the future and finding ways to ensure that we will always provide for our employee-owners and their retirement. We actively plan for future repurchase commitments. That's part of the impetus for creating both a holding company, Starfish Holdings, and Torch's sister company, Freedom Real Estate.

Above and Beyond

I've always been a big believer in incentives and their power to motivate people. It's powerful when people want to do something because they can benefit from it. When you can create an incentive that rewards both an individual and the organization they work for, then you really have something special. That's why sharing ownership with employees produces win-win results. Everyone inside the business is aligned and motivated to tackle their shared goal of building up the value of the business—together.

But we also have gone further in creating incentives to reward our top performers using stock appreciation rights (SARs).

When we started Torch, we awarded our early employees stock options in the business—all of which were cashed out by 2011. SARs work similarly to stock options, but they aren't true equity. They are what's called "synthetic" equity instead. The idea is that an employee can be awarded a certain number of SARs, which are tied to the current stock price. Then, over time (five years in our case), they will receive a bonus equivalent to the amount the stock price has increased since they were awarded the SARs.

One-third of the value of the SARs is paid out after three years, another third after year four, and the final third after year five. For example: Let's say I receive three shares of SARs where the stock price is $100. After three years, if the stock has risen to $125, I receive a bonus of $25 to pay for the SAR share that grew from $100 to $125 in those three years. The next year, if the stock goes up to $140, I receive a bonus of $40 to pay for the SAR share that grew from $100 to $140 in those four years. Then, after year five, if the stock goes up to $150, I will receive a bonus of $50 to pay for the SAR share that grew from $100 to $150 in those five years.

Everyone in the company is eligible to receive these SARs. These are intended to give another bite at the apple to our employee-owners who go above and beyond in ways that significantly impact our enterprise value. Some people might earn new SARs awards every year, meaning they can eventually earn payout bonuses each year, which can become substantial if the company's value continues to grow by 15 percent to 30 percent a year. If we can continue to grow the company's value at that pace, every employee will earn the opportunity to enjoy a successful retirement.

SARs are also an effective retention tool because they give employee-owners the incentive to stick around. If they should decide to leave before their SARs mature, they don't receive any payout. You must stay to get it.

Our SARs program, which is still in effect today, reflects a common theme in the Torch story—we drove the growth and success of the business methodically and meaningfully. We wanted people to have a stake in the outcome of the success they were creating. That was their motivation for putting in those long hours to work on proposals on nights and weekends. Everyone who put in the extra effort knew they would benefit financially—but only if the company also won. Whatever we did had to be in the best interests of the company. If we did that, then we as individuals would also win. The gains we would see would be worth all the time and effort we'd invested. We all had the motivation to go that extra mile to help push the company forward.

CHAPTER FIVE

Generosity Is a Superpower

I once picked up a plaque at a garage sale that now hangs in my home office. It features a quote from Dr. Martin Luther King, Jr. I'm amazed even today at how eloquent a speaker Dr. King was, especially compared to a rural guy like me. Sometimes I get chill bumps when I listen to recordings of him speaking. The garage sale plaque displays his quote, "The time is always right to do what is right."

In many ways, this became both a personal mantra for me and the entire business. Time and again during the first twenty years of Torch's history, we made choices—sometimes difficult ones—to keep true to the idea that doing the right thing was the best thing. Whether that was in how we treated our sub-contractors or how we kept good employees on the payroll even when we lost a contract, our default was always to do what we thought was the right thing. And we found that we were repaid many times over by those decisions—even if that wasn't ever our goal. It worked out, as Dr. King said so well, that it just made sense for us to do the right thing time and again. That's something we're all extremely proud of.

Here is what we might call "the Heart of Torch" in action. Anyone who knows me, knows that anytime I share these stories and ones like them, I tend to get choked up pretty quickly. You should know the same is true when I write them.

Giving Back

After being in business for two years, Don and I recognized it was time we developed a more organized approach to how we gave back to our community through charitable contributions. But we didn't want to have the only say as to which nonprofits or causes we should donate to. As it happened, two of our employees—Janet Haenisch and Clay Hagan—had each approached me with some ideas of how we could begin giving back to the community. So, I asked them to assist me by creating a program to help us, as a company, decide which organizations we could donate to.

Rather than coming up with a list of organizations to donate to, Janet and Clay came back to me with a proposal for a new charitable giving program that the employees would run and decide who would receive their donations. Janet and Clay had heard and fully understood the principle of what we wanted to achieve. They also knew that in our culture they were empowered to "own" and present a better solution if they had one.

Janet had seen a similar program work at her former employer, CAS, so she and Clay built our program along those lines—but with a key difference. While the "CAS Cares" program was funded with employee donations, it was run by a board who decided where the money went. Employees would learn who received it after the fact. Janet and Clay wanted to flip that script by giving every participant in the program a chance to influence where the money went.

"The traditional way of giving wasn't the way we wanted to run the company," Janet said, pointing to examples like giving money to United Way and similar organizations. "We wanted the people who participated to get to pick and choose who gets the money."

Janet took charge of governance while Clay handled the financials. Participating in the program, which soon was named "Torch Helps" when we launched it in June 2005, would be voluntary. In other words, employees could decide if they wanted to have money automatically deducted from their paycheck or not. If they did want to participate, then they would have a say, through a voting process, in whom Torch Helps provided money to.

For my part, I agreed that the company would help get the program started by covering all the administration, legal, and set-up fees to get Torch Helps off the ground as a 501(c)(3) nonprofit organization. After that, the charitable contributions would be decided by the employees. As engineers, it may not come as a surprise that Janet and Clay created a thorough screening process to help vet which organizations would be eligible to receive donations. For her part, Janet did a lot of research to understand how organizations like the Better Business Bureau rate nonprofits. They then used those same standards as part of the screening committee. They also created an electronic voting process where everyone who participated in the program could cast their ballot for whom they would like to receive funding through quarterly grants. For the first year, the goal was to raise $20,000 from the sixty-seven employees we had at the time.

Because organizations that cater to causes like therapy dogs—which Torch Helps has supported—pull on everyone's heartstrings, rules were put into place to help ensure that the grants were spread out among a diverse range of causes each year. In other words, we didn't want to have the same organizations win every year. We put a rule in place that if an organization won an award, they would have to sit out a year before they could apply for another.

It's been a remarkable ride for Torch Helps since then. I'm so proud of the impact this program—and others we have started, including the money donated by Torch directly—has had on our community. Even folks in Huntsville who might not know Torch the company might recognize the various ways our employees have given back both in terms of money and their time as volunteers over the years. Whether that involved helping fund a new public library or helping the local hospital acquire new equipment, we have been able to support the people in our community over the years. Torch Helps even caught the attention of the National Center for Employee Ownership (NCEO) and the Beyster Institute at the University of California San Diego's Rady School of Management, who gave us an Innovation in Employee Ownership Award in 2012. At the time of this writing, Torch Helps has supported more than ninety-five organizations in the community since 2005, through grants of more than $1.2 million.

Torch Helps has become an incredible asset for the company over time. Part of the reason that Torch Helps has become such a big part of the Torch culture is because of the impacts it made early on.

Helping Those in Need

In August 2005, a local TV news segment called "Crime Stoppers" featured a story about a group of local Boy Scouts from Huntsville (Troop 633) who had their trailer stolen from a church parking lot. Someone had backed up a hitch to it and took off with it in tow. The trailer was packed with all the gear the troop used for their camping trips—tents, sleeping bags, cookware, etc. They estimated the cost of all their gear to be at least $15,000. The heartbreaking thing was that those Scouts had paid for all that equipment themselves. It took them five years of selling popcorn, one dollar at a time.

Someone saw that TV segment and proposed that Torch Helps could buy the Scouts a new trailer and gear. The committee put the idea up for a vote to the employees, and it was readily accepted.

Clay then took the lead in getting as much material as they could using the funds Torch Helps had on hand. He went to the local Lowes, for example, and convinced them to sell a trailer at below-cost for the cause. It was similar in size to the ones the Scouts lost, but with more headroom and better safety features like LED lights. Clay then tapped a former colleague, Mike Alvarez, at another local company, Mil-Tec, to join us in contributing additional funds to the Scouts. Clay also reached out to Dick's Sporting Goods, who agreed to sell gear to the Scouts at a steep discount to stretch those dollars as far as possible.

Thanks to all of Clay's hard work and the employee donations, we had a trailer that the Scouts could fill up with the gear they needed to replace what they had lost. Now, it was time to come up with a creative way to give it to them. But all that had to wait, because life intervened.

Rallying for a Cause

When Hurricane Katrina struck the Gulf Coast and the city of New Orleans on August 29, 2005, the horrors of the storm hit too close to home. Huntsville is several hundred miles inland from the coast, so we avoided the worst of the storm. But so many of us had family and friends who suffered firsthand from the devastating storm.

One of those was Clayton Newkirk, who grew up in the coastal town of Waveland, Mississippi, near the Louisiana border. Katrina sent a thirty-foot wall of water crashing into the small town, devastating everything it touched. One of Clayton's childhood friends was the sheriff in Waveland, and when Clayton saw how bad things were on the news, he decided to act. "I knew I had to do something. I didn't know what," he said.

What he did was hitch up his father-in-law's utility trailer to his van and fill it with all the food, tents, clothing, gasoline, and propane tanks he could get his hands on before taking off toward the coast. It was a risky move, especially since most of the area had been declared off-limits by the National Guard, who had been called in to help. But by dropping his friend's name, Clayton got through and was able to deliver his load of supplies.

What also became clear was that those supplies were not enough to help the Waveland community—not by a long shot. Things like generators were especially needed, as the area had yet to restore power.

When Clayton returned home to Huntsville, he was already planning his return trip to Waveland. He especially wanted to find a way to get his sheriff friend a generator and some cooking supplies. But this time, he decided to call in reinforcements. After sending an email around to his Torch colleagues, many of whom quickly agreed to make donations, Clayton was reminded about the new Torch Helps program. He approached Janet and Clay with a request. He wanted to funnel any donations that people—including customers, investors, community members, and even competitors—wanted to make to the folks in Waveland.

After checking with lawyers to ensure everything was good, Clayton's request was approved. He soon had $10,000 worth of contributions to invest in more generators, chain saws, gasoline, propane tanks, and other supplies that were so desperately needed on the coast. Torch employees also assembled hundreds of care packages they sent along with Clayton to hand out to the survivors of the disaster. It was too much for him to handle alone, so Clay volunteered to join him on the return trip, driving a second van Clay had borrowed from a friend. They had to strap tanks of gas to the roofs of both vans to ensure they had enough fuel to get back home.

Clayton and Clay left on Saturday, September 3, and drove through the night to arrive in Waveland an hour or so after daybreak. They distributed the donated items, including a couple of electric generators, to people Clayton knew, all

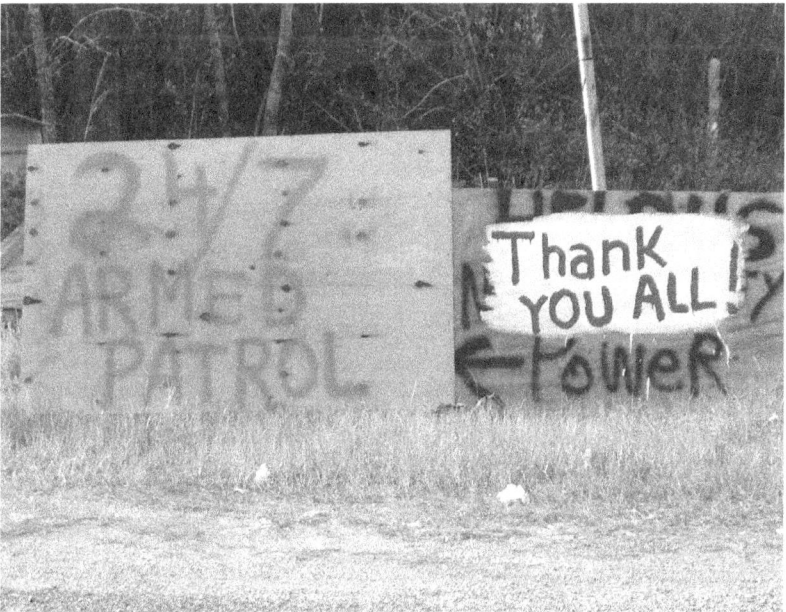

morning and into the hot afternoon. Then, they left before dark to return to Huntsville.

Clay brought a camera with him on the trip and took eighty-five photos of what he and Clayton encountered on their journey, including the two photos preceding. The first, they encountered on their way in. Clayton knew some people who lived on that road, so they dropped off a couple of portable generators. On the way back out of town after the long, hot day, they saw the sign had been updated.

"It was in that moment that Torch really felt like a family," said Clayton. "I'll be forever grateful to everyone who helped."

Scout's Honor

In October 2005, we had just moved into a new office space, and we decided to hold an open house event to celebrate with the families of our employees as well as our investors and members of the community. We also called up Boy Scout Troop 633 and asked them to provide us with traffic control for the event as a service mission. It was quite the ruse, seeing as we only had seventy-five or so employees at the time. There weren't going to be any big crowds. But they bought it and agreed to come.

We opened the event in a way that kept our cards close to the chest. By inviting their parents as well, the Scouts knew something special was planned, but they couldn't have guessed what was about to happen.

Eventually, we wheeled out the trailer and let everyone in the crowd know the real reason we had invited the boys. At first, the twenty-one Scouts—who were between twelve and fifteen years old—looked at each other and at us in disbelief. They quite literally couldn't process why a group of people they had never met before had made the effort to replace their trailer and gear. They started hugging each other and then started hugging us. It didn't take long before you couldn't find a dry eye in the house. It was a moving moment, and one that I am sure everyone who was there will never forget.

"We are just so grateful," fifteen-year-old Steven Price, senior patrol leader for Troop 633, told the *Huntsville Times*. "You see surprises like that on television shows, but you don't expect it to happen to you."[10]

Later, Clay attended a Mil-Tec–sponsored event at Dick's Sporting Goods where the Scouts went shopping for their new gear. "The one thing we told the boys was that you hear the news, you can work to change it unless it's the weather," Clay said at the time. "When we heard the news about what had happened to these Scouts, we wanted to help change it for them."

The Honor of a Lifetime

Strangely enough, the connections between Torch Helps, the Boy Scouts, and Katrina didn't end there. A few months after the hurricane, the Scouts from Troop 633 in Huntsville heard about a fellow troop in Mississippi that had lost their gear

---

10. Patricia C. McCarter, "Torch Technologies Workers Deserve a Merit Badge," *Huntsville Times*, October 4, 2005.

trailer because of the storm. Well, they immediately donated half the gear inside their trailer to those Scouts in Mississippi. We know this because they wrote us a deeply appreciative letter telling us what they did, while also thanking us for our generosity. Talk about paying it forward. As I hope you can imagine, I had a hard time not shedding a tear or two on that piece of paper. This story still chokes me up, even today.

While I recognize I might be stretching the limits of my credibility with you, the story of those Scouts doesn't even end at that emotional moment.

A few months after they received their trailer, we learned that Torch had been nominated for an award handed out by the Huntsville branch of the Better Business Bureau. The award, given annually by each regional BBB, is called the Torch Award (I'm not making this up!), and it's given to a company that exhibits outstanding business ethics. It's a big deal to be nominated, and obviously, we were incredibly honored. You had to be in business for three years to be eligible, and we were nominated on literally the day Torch turned three.

Things got even more interesting when we showed up for the awards ceremony. When they made the official announcement that we had won the Torch Award, we were completely floored. They then started reading from an essay written by one of the Scouts from Huntsville Troop 633 about his experience with the generosity of our company and how he believed we were a model of an ethical company.

Now, I was fully prepared to go up on stage and accept the award on behalf of the company and our associates. But hearing that kid's letter and the sentiment within it shook me up big time. I was so emotional, Don had to go up and accept the award.

You can't imagine the kind of recognition we received inside the community for winning that accolade. Since we pride ourselves on being an ethical company, it was incredible to be recognized by our peers and the members of the community. It's easier for me now to look back and reflect on that moment and recognize how things tend to come full circle. The more good you do, the more good gets done—it's a virtuous cycle.

Facing the Music

If you would believe it, there's yet another Torch Helps story that involves a stolen trailer. In this case, the Madison County High School band was preparing to head to a state competition when someone stole their trailer right off school grounds. It was a devastating blow to the band, which used the trailer to haul all of their equipment—marching drums, pit equipment, xylophones, bells, chimes, bass drums, and timpani—for their fifty band members to football games and other events. Now, they had no way of getting all their musical gear to their upcoming competition.

As a company, Torch bought the band a new trailer. And just as we unveiled the gift to the Scout troop, we first invited the band to perform an outdoor concert at our headquarters-for us and their family members. After they finished playing and the applause died down, we pulled out their new trailer, which featured their logo.

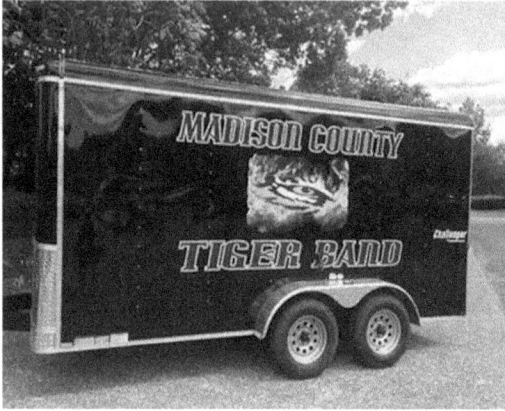

The stunned looks on those kids' faces were priceless. Just as powerful were the reactions of their parents. It wasn't long before everyone had tears in their eyes—me included. There were some news reporters on-site to capture the moment: "We did this once before and we saw so much good come out of it with the kids," I was quoted as saying. "They took it upon themselves to do good for the community beyond that, so it was a gift that just paid itself forward."[11]

Hearts of Gold

There really is something to the idea that when you do good things, more good things seem to follow. In order for Torch

---

11. Lucy Berry, "Madison County Band Celebrates Donated Trailer 2 Months after Old One Was Stolen," *Huntsville Real-Time News*, May 5, 2016.

to become 100 percent employee-owned, our early investors who helped us get off the ground had to be willing to sell their shares in the business. They all knew they were getting a great return—the stock had soared from seven cents per share to more than $2 per share. Many of those investments were now worth more than $1 million dollars.

But these folks weren't foolish. They could see how the company was progressing. If they held on to their equity, they could see it growing even faster and bigger. But they didn't. They all agreed to sell because they understood the original mission and vision of the business was to become employee-owned. They were willing to cash out and make that dream a reality (despite having to give up the chance to brag around town that they owned Torch stock).

The shocking thing, however, was how many of those investors took a good chunk of the money they earned from selling their Torch stock and donated it to organizations like churches and schools in the community. Again, we're talking about millions of dollars—life-changing sums of money—that were reinvested in great causes inside Huntsville. One investor, Bob Wills, donated every penny he made from his investment. Bob is a local entrepreneur who owns a business called Sea Wire & Cable, which is partly owned by an ESOP. He was also an investor in Torch Concepts. Bob is known to walk around town with a roll of quarters in his pocket and then go up to families and ask the kids if they have a piggy bank. If they do, they get a quarter to invest for the future. Bob is also known for investing in start-ups all over town, some of which went bust. When we cashed out Bob's stake in Torch, he donated all the money to the Randolph School, where he served on the board, to help fund a campus expansion.

When I found out what Bob had done, I asked him why he didn't at least keep some of the money for himself. "Bill," he told me, "when you make the kinds of investments like I did in Torch, you always hope to make a bit of money back. But many times, I don't. With our Torch investment, I got thirty times my investment. Well, the tax savings I'll get from donating that money will more than offset anything I could have kept for myself." But I also know that Bob was thrilled he was able to make such an incredible impact on people's lives inside the community through his donations. What a wonderful spirit! Our investors truly demonstrated to our employees the power of generosity.

The Heart of Torch

That spirit of giving back lives on at Torch. Not only does Torch Helps continue to play a vital role in our community, but we have also launched multiple other programs, such as Torch Gives (now called Torch in Action), which gives Torch's employee-owners volunteer opportunities throughout Huntsville like building wheelchair ramps and helping erect homes through Habitat for Humanity.

I personally have been involved in raising money as part of the American Heart Association's annual Heart Walk—which is tied to my own experience with having a heart attack. We can usually count on one hundred or more folks from Torch participating in the event. It's also become a bit of a competition with some of us at Torch to see who can raise the most money each year. I took some pride in leading the pack for several years.

Then, one year, as we neared the deadline, I was neck-and-neck with Debbie Overcash, who had joined Torch as an executive assistant a few years earlier. Debbie had used her abundant southern charm to steal away some of my tried-and-true donors, so I threatened to simply write a check to ensure I won. And, in the end, I did write a check—and donated it in Debbie's name to give her the win. The better person won in the end. She has won every year since.

Another organization we have supported over the years is called The Arc of Madison County. Its mission is to help care for, and create meaningful lives for, people with intellectual disabilities. Not only have we helped The Arc through donations, but we've also found ways to employ some of their residents, who are thrilled at the opportunity to make some money by using their hands.

There's also a funny personal story tied to The Arc, in what turned out to be the first formal grant issued by Torch Helps. The $5,000 grant was matched by a federal program that enabled the program's director to buy a new vehicle (I think it was a Ford Taurus) to help replace the dilapidated vehicle she was using for work. The new car would provide safe transportation for her to take folks from The Arc on doctor visits to Nashville, Tennessee; Atlanta, Georgia; and Birmingham, Alabama.

Well, one day after that, I was raking leaves in my yard when an attractive young woman pulled up to the sidewalk, ran up to me, and gave me a great big hug and a kiss on the cheek. I can only imagine what Brenda (who was standing next to me) was thinking. She happened to be holding a shovel in her hands, and things could have gotten ugly quickly! As it turned out, that young woman was The Arc's director. She was just saying thank you for the big heart of Torch. She and Brenda are great friends today, for what it's worth.

The importance of giving back to our community is tied to the fact that we are owners of the business. It's all of our jobs to ensure the city we work and play in remains as healthy as our business. That's why we also work closely with the Community Foundation to help steward our additional corporate contributions.

As Torch has grown and expanded into new geographies like Colorado and Florida, we've also expanded and found new ways to support cause-driven organizations in those communities. At times, we've even found ways to help people beyond communities where we live, like the time we found a way to support flood victims in Nashville and in Kentucky. My point in sharing these stories is that when you focus on doing the right thing, word gets around. You begin to build a culture around those stories about what you do well and when you did the right thing by others.

This has become such a strong part of the Torch story that people now want to come work for Torch because of our reputation for giving back. While I was writing this book, Brenda and I were out eating dinner at a local restaurant when a member of the community came up to say hello. She told us that she wanted to introduce us to her daughter and son-in-law, both of whom were new employees at Torch. I was thrilled to meet them both but was even more blown away when the young woman told me that she had job offers from other companies in town that came with higher salaries than what she was going to earn at Torch. But she chose Torch because she knew how much it gave back to the community. That was extremely important to her.

That young woman isn't alone. In fact, we're now seeing a second generation of Torch employees made up of the sons and daughters of those who helped build the company up from the ground floor. One great example is Brett Clark, the son of Sue Clark, Torch's CFO from 2005 to 2017 and now CFO of Starfish. Sue (along with Tina Corley, whom she took over for) has long been on me for low-balling or "sandbagging" my growth estimates for Torch. Over the years, Sue has brought her family to numerous Torch events, like company picnics and Christmas parties. That's when I first got to meet Brett—who I learned was not a fan of Santa Claus or Chuck E. Cheese.

Later, as a young adult, Brett went on to study physics and engineering at Auburn University, where he won awards for his scholarship and research. With his academic credentials, Brett could work just about anywhere he wanted. But he chose to work for Torch, where he is now a software engineer in addition to his duties at Starfish. "I didn't push him to take a job here," Sue said, who pointed out that Brett was also an Eagle Scout and active volunteer in the community. "He was considering pursuing his master's degree and other jobs. But he chose to work for Torch because it has such a strong reputation as a great place to work."[12]

It wouldn't surprise me at all if Brett was running the whole company someday. My dream is that the future of Torch is built by the next generation of employee-owners who continue to value the power of always doing the right thing.

---

12. Sue Clark, in conversation with the author, July 26, 2022.

CHAPTER SIX

Go Big or Go Home

After we had been in business for a few years, Don and I took our management team (which numbered eleven people in total at the time) to the Opryland Hotel in Nashville to hold a strategic off-site meeting. I asked one of our board members, Jim Moule, to help facilitate our discussion about how to establish our shared vision for growth. While we had been growing and doing well as a business, it was time for us to think about what we wanted to become when we "grew up."

One path we could consider would be to remain what you might call a "lifestyle" business. The idea would be to find our niche as a small business with maybe a maximum of three hundred to four hundred employees and continue to work as a subcontractor to the big service prime contractors like SAIC and CSC. (Side note: There is another category of prime contractors, such as Boeing and Raytheon, who manufacture the hardware employed by the military and government.)

The other road we could take would be to become a prime contractor ourselves. This was obviously the riskier path to take because it would bring us into direct competition with companies like SAIC and CSC, which were, at that time, massively larger than Torch.

As we discussed the pros and cons of each avenue, it became apparent that choosing to remain a subcontractor business brought its own risks as well. We couldn't control our destiny. We would be subject to the will of whatever prime contractor we were working with. They were the ones who made the decisions. If the government customer made the decision to stop some work, for example, the prime would look first to cut its subcontractors to preserve the remaining work for its own people.

We had some heated debates about the topic, but we soon arrived at a consensus: We would pursue growth and, eventually, become a prime contractor ourselves. To do that was going to take us several years of planning and strategizing about the kinds of customers to pursue and contracts to bid on. It was time to step up our game.

Here is how Jim Moule summarized our takeaways in a Strengths, Weaknesses, Opportunities, and Threats (SWOT) analysis based on that strategy session:

TORCH TECHNOLOGIES 2006 OFF-SITE MEETING

Introduction

In March of 2006, Bill Roark, Don Holder, and a number of key employees met in Nashville to establish a long-range (five-year) plan for Torch Technologies. To ensure that the conclusions represented what the employees thought, not what they thought Bill and Don wanted to hear, Jim Moule was asked to act as the facilitator.

This session produced a "SWOT" (an assessment of strengths, weaknesses, opportunities, and threats) and a prioritized list of action items. The elements of a more structured long-range plan were discussed as the first step toward developing one.

The following is a summary of the corporate SWOT assessment. Outline plans for each business area are presented in Appendix A.

Strengths

- Fair & ethical business practices
- Employees are experts in their field
- Torch balances customer, employee, & community interests
- Customer contacts
- Customer respect/good customer relationships
- Financial stability
  - Diverse customer base
  - Strong balance sheet
- Management commitment to goals & culture
  - Family atmosphere

continued

- Open door policy
- Share the wealth
- Enthusiasm
- Employees trusted to deal with customer
- Cost competitive
- ESOP company

Weaknesses

- Torch does not have the depth in personnel to handle new work coming in. Business development rate exceeds hiring rate.
- Company lacks a defined organization structure. Delegation of authority not clear.
- Administrative infrastructure stretched too thin
  - Overdependence on a few key employees
  - Timeliness of administrative actions
  - Need experienced FSO
  - Business managers need timely financial info to achieve profit goals
- Career development paths not clear
  - Promises to new employees inconsistent
  - Career path for non-managerial employees not clear (dual-track or not?)
  - Uncertainty could lead to internal competition
- Lack of prime contracts
- Need a few unique technical tools to develop new business
- Lack the capability to prepare the proposals expected in 2006 & 2007

- Bill and Don stretched too thin. No contingency plan for the incapacity of either.

- Employees spread all over—most off-site. Communication is difficult.

- Ability to get early warning and react rapidly to market changes

Opportunities

In each of Torch's present business areas, Torch has the potential of doubling or tripling in five years through progressive engagement.

Over and above that, there are opportunities to increase revenues another tenfold through competitive procurements that can be identified now. One of these, a modeling and simulation procurement in Ron Davis's area, was discussed in this session. Two others, SETAC and JT&E, were not.

Above and beyond that, Torch has the potential of generating additional revenues over the next five years by supporting other government agencies in Huntsville. Marshall Space Flight Center and MSIC are examples.

Threats

- Demand for qualified personnel in Huntsville exceeds supply

- Maintaining Torch's current, cooperative culture as Torch grows

Top Five Prioritized Actions

1. Form a task group to define and implement an enhanced hiring process.

2. Define Torch's organizational structure.

3. Bulk up Torch's administrative infrastructure.

continued

> 4. Create a proposal development machine.
>
> 5. Define managerial and non-managerial career paths within Torch including guidelines on option grants.
>
> Additionally, focus group meetings should be held to develop a strategy for each present business area and for each major new competitive opportunity in more depth than was possible in this off-site.

A Missed Opportunity

In 2006, Don and I were approached by Booz Allen Hamilton, one of the prime contractors. They told us they had been hearing good things about us and they encouraged us to bid on our first prime small business contract. They convinced us we were a shoo-in to win.

For any readers who don't work in government contracting, responding to a government request for proposal (RFP) and making a bid for the project takes an incredible amount of work. In those days, the amount of paper in a proposal could fill the back of a pickup truck. There are often multiple sections covering everything from the technical aspects of the project to the accounting and software elements, to say nothing about the cost volume. If you want to put together a winning proposal, you need to prove to the customer that you can handle all their requirements—for a lower price than your competitors. You can't cash a check if you come in second.

As you might imagine, completing the proposal process takes an incredible effort. One person alone can't write it.

Working on these proposals takes so much effort, in fact, that back in the Nichols days, we'd seen families split apart over the stress and time away from home. It's a real challenge to find a work-life balance when tackling a proposal.

At this point in Torch history, though, we didn't have a dedicated "proposal team" to tackle the work. It was up to us. So, after many of us worked our eight hours over at the Arsenal during the day, we set up shop at night or on the weekend inside our war room to complete the proposal. I had a solid track record of winning bids on proposals back in my days at Nichols, so I took the lead on this proposal team, leaning on just a few other early Torch employees for help. That involved a lot of late nights—and a lot of Diet Cokes—to get all the work done. It just about killed us.

In the case of this first attempt at winning a prime contract, we were going to bid on a project that was set aside for a small business to win. We thought it was the perfect kind of project for us to begin building momentum with.

Yet, when the government announced the winner, we learned we had lost. Worse, we finished dead last. It felt like a real setback to everyone. That was especially true for me, since I had won something like ten contracts in a row dating back to my Nichols days. I felt humiliated. It would been easy to tuck my tail between my legs and change course after that. But I did something different.

When you lose out on a contract, the government provides what's called a "debrief" where they explain why you lost. I dutifully showed up at our debrief and did my best to show my humility and desire to learn how we could do better the next time. I apologized for wasting everyone's time. I took copious notes and expressed a lot of appreciation for the education in how we could get better. Fortunately for us, we got a lot of insights from that debrief—all of which we tucked away to help us win future bids.

Perhaps just as importantly, we were able to hire two new employees who couldn't work for the bid-winning company due to a conflict of interest. Also because of that loss, we eventually landed a long-time customer who was involved in the debrief session. Apparently, we impressed them with our humility and desire to improve, so they gave us a shot to work for them.

Picking Ourselves Back Up

A year later, we decided to take another shot at winning a prime contract. But we were going to tackle the proposal process differently.

First off, we were going to get more people involved in the process. One of the mistakes we made in our first attempt was not utilizing the breadth of expertise and experience of our people to make the strongest bid, especially on the technical elements of the work. There is an art to writing a good proposal. That's especially true when you get a large team involved like we were about to do. You still need to have someone pull everything together and then help edit everything so all the writing is consistent. To do all this well, you need a team effort.

The second move we took was to hire Ron Patrick, who had run the proposal center at Nichols, to consult with us on how to approach the proposal process more effectively. I also asked Clay Hagan to shadow Ron and learn everything he could, since he would lead our proposal teams going forward. Clay remembers me telling everyone that when it came to proposals, everyone in the company worked for Ron. Including me. If he wanted a printer moved, we would get it done. Ron would have top priority.

Ron was famous in his Nichols days for his adherence to discipline and deadlines. One time, Don was involved in rebidding on a proposal for incumbent work. Ron's rule was that as soon as the technical team delivered their work to the proposal team, no further changes were allowed. None. No excuses whatsoever. But Don and Anita Wood (who would also later join Torch) found an error in the work they had turned in. Not a typo, but something major that they thought would put the proposal in jeopardy. There were still two days before the proposal was due, so they requested to make the change. It didn't matter: Ron refused to let them alter anything. He told them they missed their deadline. And that was that. In the end, the team won the contract anyway. But it sent a clear message to everyone that Ron wasn't going to tolerate any deviation from the rules. And he was now bringing that discipline to Torch. Later, we would bring in another proposal expert, Bill Gray, to tap his similar expertise.

We then leveraged our revised and revamped proposal team approach to bid on our next prime contract. The improvements were evident, and we put together a strong package. But we still lost. It was close, though—really close. We lost by something like one-tenth of one percent on cost. Some of us thought perhaps we should have ranked more highly on our technical merits—which could have given us grounds to protest the win—but we decided to lick our wounds instead. One of the principles I wanted us to always adhere to was to treat our customers with respect with the hope they would return the favor in kind.

Making a Big Bet

Despite the bad news of losing our second prime contract attempt in a row, things weren't all bad in the business. While we had missed on our big swings, we had still grown Torch to about $20 million in annual revenue based on our continued work on various projects as a subcontractor. That was an impressive enough growth rate for *Inc.* magazine to award us the rank of No. 818 on its 2007 Inc. 5000 list, which highlights the fastest-growing companies in the country. (We would go on to make this rankings list fifteen years in a row, one of only four companies to earn that honor.) Torch was also named the fastest-growing private defense contractor in the Southeast and No. 8 in the Defense Contractors category. For context, that was the same year Apple's iPhone made its debut.

Winning this award was a big deal for our young company, so Don and I decided to attend the Inc. 5000 conference in Chicago in September of that year. We brought our wives to make it a fun getaway. It was exciting to be part of a crowd of entrepreneurs who were growing businesses. Former President Bill Clinton was one of the speakers at the conference. But it was another speaker who really grabbed my attention.

It was Jim Collins, the Stanford University professor and prolific author. His book *Good to Great* remains required reading for any entrepreneur even now, more than twenty years after it was first published. At the conference, Collins spoke about the concept of how great companies should have a "big, hairy, audacious goal" (or BHAG for short). In *Good to Great*, Collins writes that a BHAG is "a big and daunting goal—like a mountain to climb."[13] At the same time, it's also something everyone in the company understands right away and is inspired to tackle. Like with the NASA Moon mission, it brings everyone together in pursuit of something remarkable.

That was inspiring stuff for me. While we were still licking our wounds from losing those two initial attempts to win contracts as a small business prime, we could set our sights even higher. Maybe we should try to win a contract as a true prime—where we go up against the other primes like CSC and SAIC. That would certainly be big, hairy, and audacious!

I was still chewing on this notion after we returned to Huntsville when Ron Davis, one of our employees, dropped another book on my desk. This one was titled *The Breakthrough Company*. "You need to read this, Bill," Ron told me.

---

13. Jim Collins, *Good to Great: Why Some Companies Make the Leap and Others Don't* (New York: HarperBusiness, 2001), 197–204.

The book's author was Keith McFarland, a former CEO and business consultant. He modeled his book after *Good to Great* and spent five years researching more than seven thousand companies that had made the Inc. 500 list since its debut in 1982 (it expanded from 500 to 5000 companies in 2007). He then highlighted the companies that had "broken through" to become billion-dollar businesses. One of the case studies in McFarland's book was Adtran, a maker of networking and communications equipment, which also happens to be based in Huntsville.

One of the common themes McFarland found when he studied the breakthrough companies was that at one time in their history, each of them had placed what he called "a big bet" to take their company to the next level.[14] Companies like Adtran recognized that they could have stayed small and played it safe. But they also recognized how that strategy came with risks as well—risks that someone else would grab their market and force them out, or that by not growing, they could lose key people who wanted to hitch their careers to a rocket ship rather than a horse and buggy. In that context, making the big bet wasn't about taking on risk, it was about making a calculated wager on the fortune of the business.

After I finished McFarland's book, I was convinced it was time for us to up the ante and make a play to become a true prime contractor. While we as a team had continued to debate

---

14. Keith McFarland, *The Breakthrough Company* (New York: Crown Currency, 2009), 55–89.

whether we should be a lifestyle or a growth company, it became clear to me that keeping the status quo carried risks as well. Eventually, even small business contractors can become targets of the primes. You're always in their power, and I was tired of that dynamic. If I could convince the team to join me, we were going to go all in. I thought it was our opportunity to go big or go home.

It Takes a Village

When I got the chance to pitch the idea of taking another swing at a prime contract, my Torch colleagues were on board. The BHAG I laid out—that we would make the big bet of becoming a real prime—inspired fire and passion among everyone. They wanted to go for it. What we didn't know was how hairy and audacious things were going to get.

As it turned out, the government was bidding a series of eight substantial task orders under the EXPRESS contract. We're talking about hundreds of millions of dollars of work at stake. That was our opportunity to swing for the fences. And it was a big swing because the scope of technical capabilities involved with the work on those contracts was significant. There was one problem: Torch was not a prime contractor on EXPRESS.

However, the EXPRESS contract had a governmental rule that allowed an EXPRESS prime to sponsor a team member to lead a task order. This was different from joining a team as a subcontractor led by a prime. We wanted to lead the bid, but we needed help. So, we started asking around to see where we could get some traction.

At first, we were stymied. In some of our conversations with the EXPRESS primes, they agreed to sponsor us on a task order or two—but only if we were a subcontractor to them on other specific task orders. Of course, they wanted us as subcontractors on the task orders we thought we had the strongest case to win as prime, and they would only sponsor us to prime the ones they felt they could not win anyway.

Finally, after several conversations with AMS, a joint venture between Camber and Dynetics, they eventually agreed to sponsor us. (We later learned that not everyone at Dynetics supported this decision. They saw us as a potential threat. But Marc Bendickson, the CEO, overruled them, saying he would rather be inside the tent with us than compete against us.)

But there was a catch: AMS said we had to bid on all eight task orders. That seemed like an incredible leap for us to make—especially because most of the contracts were "full and open," which meant that anyone, including the large business primes, could bid on them. Only one of the task orders was a small business set aside. That meant we would have to go up against the big boys if we wanted to win. It seemed like a lot of risk to take on.

And that was before we learned that the government was in the middle of changing the rules for how companies could team up with each other. In the past, there really wasn't much risk if you lost a bid. You could always make the case to the winning company about how you could add some expertise to the project, and they would add you to their team as a subcontractor. As a result of several high-profile scandals involving other government contractors, the government wasn't going to allow anyone who bid on these contracts to join another team if they lost.

This was a massive change, and it ratcheted up the stakes substantially. It meant that if we decided to go ahead and bid on these task orders, we were truly betting the company on winning these contracts. If we lost, we would likely have to shut the doors because we wouldn't have much work left. There was no safety net. The Torch story would come to an end.

But that's not what happened.

Making It into Prime Time

When the announcement was made, we were hoping to win one of the task orders. But we soon learned that we had won four of the task orders—three of which were full and open, meaning we had beaten the large primes. The implications of this upset win were staggering. Up until that point, we had grown the company to about $20 million in annual revenue. We now had contracts in hand that gave us the potential to earn $443 million over the next five years. Our big bet had paid off—big time.

It took an incredible team effort by so many Torch employees who volunteered their time after hours and on weekends to attack the countless details we had to address in bidding on these task orders. Forty or more people took part in the proposal process, which served as a model for us going forward. We would now always take a very inclusive approach to proposals. It became a way for Torch to show off the wide range of technical skills and experience from our employee-owners. Our proposal teams are part of the special sauce that has made Torch so successful.

But our winning streak didn't end there. Less than a week after winning the first task order, the government announced their intention to hold a small business open season to add new EXPRESS primes! They released the request for proposal (RFP) just six weeks after we won the first task order. If we won an EXPRESS prime, we would not need a sponsor for future bids. The timing couldn't have worked out better. The timing was so good that we began to call it "Torch Luck" or, as Clay likes to call it, "the fragility of six weeks." If the government had released the EXPRESS RFP just six weeks earlier, then we likely could not have formed our team to be credible for the bid. In retrospect, those six weeks proved to be critical in Torch being able to bid for our next major contract, which we won in 2011. That, in turn, proved to be critical in winning the OASIS contracts in 2014.

We had established enough credibility by winning that task order that we could bid on and win this top-level contract—something we would not have been qualified to do if we hadn't won those task orders just weeks earlier. We now had sufficient "past performance," as the government calls it, to qualify. As luck would have it, we won the second of four task orders and executed enough work on it that it too could be used for our top-level EXPRESS bid.

The result was that Torch Technologies was about to kick off an incredible rocket ship ride of growth, a complete turnaround from where we had been after losing our earlier efforts to win prime contracts. We didn't have to play "Mother, May I?" with the primes anymore. We would now be able to pitch our ideas directly to the customer. So many times, we'd seen primes benefit from our idea generation. Those days were over. We also encouraged other small businesses to team up with us because we wouldn't take advantage of them. We were truly looking to build partnerships. We were about to evolve from a truly small business into something much, much bigger.

But we didn't know there were going to be some bumps along the way.

CHAPTER SEVEN

A Time of Disruption

When I made my first pitch to Don, we both knew that he was planning to retire within five years. Don decided to stay for six. After our big contract wins in 2008, which put our company's growth on an entirely new trajectory, it made sense for Don to step away. He had done what he had set out to do—to help build the kind of company that was going to take care of his people.

Don was also in a good position to step away and enjoy more time with his wife, Judy. He had already retired from the government earlier in his career, and he had a healthy 401(k). But we also allowed Don to keep his shares in the company instead of selling them. As a result, he was able to benefit from the incredible growth in the stock we experienced through 2011, when the ESOP bought out all the remaining shares and stock options held by founders like the two of us. We also asked Don to remain a member of the board and to use his vast experience to continue guiding and coaching the company going forward.

Don was able to leave Torch on a high note, which was an experience totally different from events that had unfolded at his prior employers. He was retiring with dignity. At the same time, it was emotional for the rest of us—especially those who had been working with Don since the Nichols days. We wanted to do something to celebrate Don in style.

Don is a great businessperson, family man, and an amazing and gifted artist. He has a studio inside his house. I remember seeing truly beautiful portraits of his family he created using watercolors. That became our inspiration to honor Don.

The company bought an original print from a well-known regional artist, donated it to our local art museum, the Huntsville Museum of Art, and dedicated it to Don and Judy. We then threw Don a retirement party inside the museum as well. It was a bittersweet moment. While Don will always be an integral part of the Torch Technologies story, we were beginning a new chapter in the company's history without him.

A Loss in the Family

A year after Don retired, we were forced to experience a different kind of loss. In this case, and through no fault of our own, we had to sell part of the company.

The story began back in 2005 when we were working for Boeing, one of the largest defense contractors. This was different for us because our primary customers are government agencies. The ethics rules at the time stated that any company that wanted to work for the government as well as a private sector company like Boeing had to create a "firewall" that separated the business to avoid any conflicts of interest.

We took this idea of a firewall very seriously. We had seen how situations like this in the past had caused problems at companies, especially if the rules changed. So, we decided to create a separate company, Torch Systems, to tackle the work with Boeing. Torch Systems would have its own profit and loss statement and make all its business decisions independently. But the twenty-eight employees who worked at Torch Systems would still be part of the ESOP that owned Torch Technologies.

Torch Systems thrived. They grew the business to include prime contractors such as Raytheon, among others. Torch Systems soon accounted for one-sixth of the entire company's revenue—and one-third of its profits. It was proving to be a nice growth company on its own.

But at the end of 2008, the government changed the rules. Having a firewall wasn't enough anymore. The new rules stated that no contractor could work for the government and a private sector company simultaneously. Even though we had created Torch Systems as a separate entity, the fact that they were part of the same ESOP as Torch Technologies would cause problems. We were left with no choice. We had to either shut down the company (likely laying off the employees) or find someone willing to buy it. And we only had six months to make it happen.

Neither choice was appealing. I had known many of the folks from Torch Systems for years—some of them dating back to our days at Nichols. The last thing I wanted to do was shut the business down and lay people off. At the same time, I was concerned that even if we could find a buyer for the business, they wouldn't have access to the same opportunity to own a stake in the outcome of the business like they had with Torch. But that sparked an idea.

I reached out to our friends at Eastside Partners, the same folks who had helped us with our ESOP transaction involving Torch Concepts. I wanted to do something similar for Torch Systems. We would essentially give them the opportunity to buy themselves out with financing from Eastside. They would also create their own ESOP, which would pay back the loan over five years. At that point, Torch Systems would become 100 percent employee-owned.

The catch was that I had to get my board to approve the deal, because selling the company to the employees meant we weren't going to get top dollar back. I had to persuade the board on the fact that doing it this way and putting Torch Systems on a path to becoming employee-owned was consistent with Torch's initial purpose. Fortunately, the board agreed and approved the decision. It was a complicated transaction, especially because we also had to help Torch Systems—which was to be renamed nLogic—relocate to a new facility and build additional infrastructure to cover areas like benefits and HR. But we pulled it off.

Tim Thornton became the new CEO at nLogic, and he and his team (Tina Corley joined in a role similar to what she did at Torch as a part-time CFO and board member) have never looked back. They first made the Inc. 5000 list on their own in 2010, and they've earned a spot on the list just about every year since. While nLogic and Torch have no business relationship, I stay in touch with Tim often enough to know that their culture sounds like the one we have at Torch, which thrills me to no end. To me, it proves that the model we developed is not only successful, but replicable in different organizations.

A Tragic Misunderstanding

Rapidly growing the company in the wake of winning those big prime contracts in 2008 brought its fair share of stress as well. We were ambitious and competitive, but that also came with a toll on that elusive work-life balance. Late nights were the norm—especially when it came time to bid a new proposal. Even with Clay leading the proposal teams, we were constantly running hard. I didn't yet realize there was going to be a personal price to pay for setting such an aggressive pace.

In the fall of 2009, we were given the opportunity to bid on an EXPRESS task order entitled "Aerodynamics," which was held by our friends at Dynetics. By 2008, Dynetics had become a large business, and by June of 2009, AMS (a subsidiary of Dynetics) had also become a large business prime on EXPRESS. It appeared that the government intended to limit the recompete of the Aerodynamics task order to small businesses.

As a newly awarded EXPRESS small business prime, we began to form a team. We approached Dynetics, but they declined. Next, we approached Aerodyne, one of our three core team members on EXPRESS, which was also an incumbent team member on the Dynetics task order. They declined. We then assumed that AMS was going to sponsor Aerodyne (a small business) for the recompete. Five or more of the other incumbent subcontractors on the current Dynetics task order were not invited to be on the team that AMS was forming for the recompete.

Those companies all came to Torch, asking us to prime. Well before Dynetics and Aerodyne had declined to be on our team, we had signed teaming agreements with the other incumbent companies. Normally, I would never have gone up against Dynetics because of our history with them. I personally count many of their management team as personal friends. They even helped us win our first prime contracts. However, we found ourselves competing against them. And we lost.

We had put together an excellent proposal, and everyone, including me, was disappointed. That went double for the team of subcontractors (subs) we had put together to bolster our team. Some of our subs were so upset over losing this contract that they began to push us to protest it. That's the process where a losing company can petition the customer to reconsider their decision. Our team of subs didn't think Dynetics should have been able to bid for a small business contract. It was a bit of a technicality, but the subs and even some Torch employees pushed me hard to pursue the protest. Clay Hagan and I met with the government ombudsman to discuss the award.

Normally, an ombudsman will listen and calmly let you know that you do not have a good case for a protest. I felt meeting with the ombudsman would help me and Clay tell the subs that we had tried, but we could not push it any further. However, for the first time in either of our careers, the ombudsman told us we would likely win a protest if we filed it!

This began to tear me up inside. In my heart, I didn't want to do it. But I also felt an obligation to the people we had teamed with. I wanted to do the right thing. But I wasn't quite sure what that was in this situation. The stress of deciding either way started keeping me up at night. I wasn't sleeping, and I started feeling terrible. I owed those guys a lot, and the decision overwhelmed me. I just couldn't deal with it.

One morning, I was feeling especially bad, but drove to the office anyway. At some point, we were discussing the potential of protesting, and I started feeling lightheaded. So, I asked everyone to leave and closed the door to my office to try to clear my head. One of the dumbest moves I ever made. Fortunately, my office assistant knocked on my door and came in to check on me.

"Oh my God, Bill, you look sick," she said. "Are you okay?"

I did my best to laugh it off, saying, "Well your saying it that way doesn't make me feel really good."

She didn't laugh.

"Bill, we need to get you to the emergency room," she said.

I decided not to fight her on that. But she was a lot shorter than me, and I outweighed her by about a hundred pounds. Feeling as dizzy as I was, there was no way I could count on her catching me if I fell. "Get Scott," I told her, referring to Scott Parker, whom I recruited away from CSC to serve as chief operating officer of Torch. Scott is six-foot-three and a couple hundred pounds-plus, so I knew if I fell, he could drag me to the hospital. Scott somehow got me to his car and whisked me to the ER.

It wasn't long before they had me hooked up to machines, drawing blood to test whether I had experienced a heart attack. While they waited for the results, the doctor recommended I spend the night in the hospital.

I remember telling Brenda, who had driven right over, that I had left my car in the parking lot, which was in a bad part of town at the time. I asked her to call Jaye Bass so he could drive it home. Meanwhile, when I looked at my messages and emails (I had a BlackBerry at that time), everything in my inbox concerned the protest. The deadline was that evening, and everyone wanted answers. Well, wouldn't you know it, all those machines I was hooked up to started blaring—signaling that my heart was "coding," or going into cardiac arrest. Brenda reached over and snatched the phone out of my hand. That was the last I saw of it for the next three months. Brenda put the phone on lockdown.

Because of the way I left the office, I never thought to delegate the decision over the protest. If we were going to do it, it needed to be filed by midnight. As time was running out, Clay (our EXPRESS project manager) called the ombudsman and told him we were not going to protest, and asked the ombudsman if he could attempt to make internal government changes to ensure the technicality did not happen again in the future. The ombudsman said he would and that he understood our decision not to protest. The deadline came and went, and we never filed the protest. God made the decision for me. He bailed me out.

A Culture of Caring

I was out of the office for the next six weeks after my trip to the hospital. I probably should have taken longer, but I have always felt a sense of obligation to my colleagues and to the company. I have also been called a workaholic more than once. But I am a firm believer that you should never ask anyone to do something you aren't willing to do yourself. It was time for me to get back to work.

One day at 5 p.m., I turned the corner from my office to walk to the proposal room as I had so many times. The team was coming together after hours, as we had done since the first days of the company, to continue working on landing some new business. But as I was about to step into the room, Steve Haenisch and Clay Hagen blocked my way. They told me they didn't need me. "We've got this, Bill. You've taught us everything we need to get the job done. We need you to be alive and not killing yourself to stay here."

I was stunned. And, quite frankly, angry. I stomped back to my office and stewed for a bit. They were kicking me out of my own meeting! But as I sat there, my blood pressure stabilized, and I realized something: They were right. They were looking out for me, trying to protect me from myself. I'd be lying if I said I didn't shed a tear or two when I recognized how much that gesture meant to me. Ironically, our winning percentage on proposals went up without me. I was holding them back.

Brenda was thrilled when I showed up back at home—early (at least for me). I haven't worked on a proposal since. Yes, I review them, but only during working hours. That was a key moment in finding more of a work-life balance.

Struggling Back

Unfortunately, as much progress as I made in trying to work less, my heart was still having issues. I had another episode—not quite a heart attack—in December 2012. After my prior experience, I knew not to mess around this time—I went right to the hospital. The doctors told me I would need another operation, and it was going to be invasive. I begged the doctor to postpone the surgery until after Christmas. I made that doctor tear up when I told him how important it was for me to spend the holidays with my family. The good news was that I felt I could trust him after that; he showed he was truly a caring person.

The surgery went well, and I was able to go home early. Unfortunately, a few months after the surgery, I breathed in some mulch working in the yard and contracted an infection that also took me out for a while. It almost took me out for good.

Later, I felt something weird in my heart, and I found out I was not responding to antibiotics—something I had no clue about at the time. I was bedridden for days as the doctors tried to figure out how to save me. Finally, one doctor, who couldn't have stood more than five feet high (he had to stand on a stool to examine me), used advanced genomics to create a custom antibiotic to save my life. I had a long road to recovery; I had to take that drug intravenously with Brenda's help every day for almost eight weeks before I could kick the infection. I now carry a card with me to let emergency personnel know that regular antibiotics won't work on me.

The Spirit of Ownership

Another profound thing happened to me while I was in the hospital that second time. I met Carlos.

While I was in Huntsville Hospital (a place to which I owe a true debt of gratitude for saving my life, twice!), I was told that the only way they would let me leave was if I could walk two miles a day. In my case, that was the equivalent of making twenty-eight laps around the sixth-floor cardiac care unit each day. Since I really wanted to get out of there, I started as soon as I could. But it took me a while to build up the strength I needed, oftentimes getting up in the wee hours of the morning to hobble along the hallway.

One day, I noticed an employee of the hospital, who also was up in the wee hours, cleaning and polishing the floors. It was Carlos. Every time I neared him, he'd have to stop what he was doing, hop down off his machine, and towel off the floor so that I wouldn't slip and fall. I apologized to him, letting him know that I didn't mean to disrupt his work. "I'm sorry for getting in your way," I told him.

But Carlos answered me with a smile. "Not a problem," Carlos would say. "I'm just happy to see you making another lap. My job is to help keep you safe so you can go home."

I was really impressed with Carlos's attitude. Carlos owned the outcome and not just the activity he was doing. He knew that the purpose of the cardiac care unit was to get people healthy and out the door. To that end, he kept a spotless floor. But his attitude was also contributing to the positive health outcome of every patient who walked through that hallway.

After I got home, I wrote a thank-you note to the CEO of the hospital and mentioned many of the doctors, nurses, medical technicians, and Carlos. I would later find out that Carlos had been Employee of the Year for the hospital the previous year. This exceptional attitude and job performance were just an everyday thing for Carlos. He believed, and rightfully so, that he would help everyone who passed him, every day.

I asked Carlos to walk with me at the Heart Walk—and there he was, with his positive attitude and smile! I will never forget him.

I always thought every Torch employee should be inspired by Carlos. As employee-owners, everyone needed to own the outcome and not just perform an activity until the day passed. We needed to hold ourselves accountable to perform above routine expectations. We needed to make our customers happy and successful. Most everyone would have been happy if Carlos just kept the floor clean. But by rising above, he became an important part of the recovery process of many patients, just like the nurses and doctors. Management didn't delegate or mandate this kind of accountability. Carlos created it himself because he cared about the outcome of what he was doing.

I actually wrote up a version of this story and sent it out to the company with the hope that it would inspire Torch employees to capture a bit of that spirit as they worked each day. Despite our tremendous success, I didn't want anyone to take that for granted. We needed to continue to create a culture where people were focused on the outcome. A culture where we performed above expectations by choice, while delivering uncommon results. I knew if we could do that, we could create the kind of culture that was meaningful, fulfilling, and would last over the long term.

An Eye on the Future

I share these stories because not only was I humbled by these experiences, but they also marked a turning point in the Torch story. As we moved past our tenth anniversary, it became all too clear to me that we needed to understand how we could continue to get everyone rowing in the same direction toward the kind of future we wanted to build together. In other words, we needed to rely on our strategic planning process more than ever.

CHAPTER EIGHT

Charting Our Future

By bidding on (and eventually winning) those initial EXPRESS task orders in 2007, we were putting Torch on a new growth trajectory. Now that we were turning a new page in the Torch story with Don nearing retirement, we needed to scale up our team even further—fast.

While bidding on those big contracts created enormous risk, it also was proof that Torch was more than just an anonymous start-up. We were clearly going places as an organization. We began earning a reputation as a bold company filled with talented people and a mission to take care of those people by making them owners in the business. That combination of factors meant Torch was becoming an even more attractive place to work, especially for people we knew and recruited but who had stayed at companies like CSC because of various factors like stock options or because they weren't ready to make the jump to a risky start-up.

One of those was Scott Parker. I had met Scott back in 1986 at Nichols, where Scott eventually became the head of human resources (HR). Scott and I worked closely at Nichols over the years, especially as we each played a role in growing the business from about three hundred employees (when we started) to right at three thousand (when CSC acquired the business).

I had a lot of respect for Scott based on our long working relationship. When Don and I started Torch, Scott was one of the first people I tried to recruit. But Scott had an attractive compensation package and stock options at CSC, plus, as he told me, he couldn't afford the pay cut at that time to join Torch. I can smile now when I share that we asked many of our people, including other future executives like John Watson and Brad Walker, "How much of a pay cut can you afford to take?" Even though we were growing, our resources remained tight. What convinced people to join us over time was the culture—and the potential upside of ownership in stock options and, eventually, the ESOP.

But if we were ever going to fulfill our mission of creating a comfortable retirement for our employees who committed to the Torch journey, we needed a plan.

To be fair, before we won those prime contracts in 2008, we had already gathered as a leadership team multiple times to try to chart our path for growth. But those meetings weren't always productive. Often, Don and I walked away shaking our heads and wondering whether we had wasted everyone's time, since the main purpose seemed to involve everyone airing whatever gripes they had.

Those meetings often involved quite a bit of animated debate and the pounding of fists on tables. I remember how Joe Hill and I would get after each other—just about yelling—about how we could grow customer accounts by moving our employees around (something we came to call "pluck-and-place"). Joe, who was always a true champion for our customers, even threatened to quit the company if that became part of our strategy for growth. We just had very different opinions about how we could get where we wanted to go. (Joe eventually became the master of pluck-and-place.)

A big part of the problem was that these meetings often involved me pitching the team an aggressive growth strategy and having it thrown back in my face. I would spend days putting together a fifty-page document filled with competitive data and SWOT charts, plotting out the strengths, weaknesses, opportunities, and threats I saw ahead of us. When I shared that with the leadership team, I wanted their input and insights. But it seemed everyone was more comfortable "sandbagging" it—shooting for a lower goal and beating it as opposed to reaching for something potentially uncomfortable but feasible. If I mapped out a plan to show how we could grow 30 percent or even 35 percent in the next year, inevitably someone would push back—often hard—saying that there was no way we could grow that much. They truly didn't think that was achievable. Even when I tried to show them step by step how we could get there, someone wouldn't buy in.

This was tough for me because I was confident that we could grow that fast—with a goal of growing the value of our company for our shareholders in the ESOP. But getting buy-in from the team was critical to making it happen. The last thing I wanted to do was go to the board with my plan, knowing that everyone on the team thought of it as "Bill's plan" and not theirs. I knew that was a recipe for failure.

Which brings me back to Scott Parker. The pitch I made to Scott in late 2007 was that he would come into Torch as our chief administration officer (CAO). At that point, we had an administrative staff of about five people, including a human resources officer, and I wanted Scott to run that group as well as handle all the non-financial operations as a manager. At that point, Torch had grown to 126 people. Scott and I had both seen "infrastructure" treated almost as a "necessary evil" in our time at Nichols Research. The fast growth of the business put enormous pressure on the administrative and operations staff, who often had to log seventy to eighty hours a week just to try to keep up. That led to high turnover in those areas—and earned that part of the company a reputation as a kind of sweatshop. I didn't want Torch to fall into that same trap, which is why I needed Scott's help.

One of the first tasks I assigned Scott was to revamp the entire policy manual at Torch. While Janet Haenisch had done what she could by cobbling together our handbook in our early days, we now needed policies and procedures that integrated across operational areas and were written to withstand legal challenges. Scott thought he would need about six months to get the project completed. Scott delivered, but we also never stopped writing and improving policies over the years.

Just as importantly, I asked Scott to help us build the kind of internal systems and communications infrastructure we would need to scale and fulfill our goal of becoming a growth company. I was going to need Scott's help to get everyone on the same page. That would prove easier said than done.

Spirited Debate

It turned out that Scott and I got into some epic debates ourselves about the direction of the company and my strategic plan. Scott also had to balance what he was hearing from Don, but that didn't make it any easier for me. Scott, who is a very tall man, would come and stand across from me while I sat at my desk. His hands were propped behind his head against the wall as we traded arguments with each other. We had a lot of respect and trust for each other, but those were some animated discussions!

Sometime later, I noticed some dark spots on the wall of my office, almost like the paint had been rubbed off. I called Scott into my office and asked him to take his usual stance across from my desk. Sure enough, the spots on the wall lined up exactly with where Scott's hands landed on the wall.

More Than a Minute

Several months later, fortune (or Torch Luck) smiled upon us once again. I had joined Vistage, the executive networking group, to get access to best practices used by other companies. Torch was the only defense contractor in the peer group, which was great in that we could access a diversity of thought concerning how we could best run and grow our business.

In March 2008, I was supposed to attend a Vistage event in Birmingham. But something came up, and I sent Scott in my place. Who knows how things would have worked out if I had gone instead. But Scott attended a session at the event hosted by Holly Green, who was a president at the Ken Blanchard Company. In her session, Holly—who had worked with companies like Xerox, Coca-Cola, and Microsoft—discussed her approach to strategic planning and goal setting, which she had written a book about, titled *More Than a Minute*.

"She spoke for ninety minutes out of a nine-hour day," said Scott. "And that was the most engaging ninety minutes I had ever sat through. She was an unbelievable speaker."[15]

After Scott read Holly's book, he was hooked. He became convinced that her system and approach to getting everyone on the same strategic page was exactly what we needed at Torch. But there was a catch.

"I knew that if I or Bill tried to teach Holly's system, we'd never get buy-in from the team," said Scott. "I knew in my heart they'd need to hear it from her directly."

---

15. Scott Parker, in conversation with the author, September 1, 2022.

But Holly charged something like $10,000 a day to coach companies—a sum that was unbelievably large for Torch's budget at the time. To his credit, Scott didn't relent. He kept pushing me to open the company wallet to hire her. Eventually, after Holly agreed to give us a discount (it still amounted to more money than we had spent on training for the prior two years combined), we brought her in for a couple of days. Torch hasn't been the same since.

Building Buy-in

A key goal of our first session with Holly, which we held at NASA's Space & Rocket Center in Huntsville, was for her to help us develop an honest assessment of where the organization stood. We had done some pre-work for her within our different areas of the business, giving her a sense of the organizational chart and responsibilities, as well as our initial SWOT analysis. We also shared our struggles with getting buy-in to the strategic goals and numbers I thought we should be aiming for.

I can admit now that I was a bit stubborn about this whole topic. I would keep bringing it up every year, mapping out all of the opportunities I thought we had in front of us, and the team would fight back each and every time, telling me my goals were too ridiculously high. I was going through the process alone and then announcing the plan to the troops. The plan I presented was aggressive, and getting buy-in from the leadership was difficult if not impossible. We were struggling to agree.

The simple process we used to grow our company at our fast pace, along with the fact that our employees are owners, provides the map and the motivation to achieve incredible results.

When Holly came in that day, she gave me very specific instructions. She told me to sit in the back of the room and not to say a word as the team went through her planning process. I started to protest until I saw she meant business. I threw up my hands in mock surrender and sat back to watch the show.

A Plan Emerges

With Holly's guidance, the team took a deep dive into understanding where we wanted to go as a company within our rapidly growing and changing industry. To help frame the challenge, she shared an excerpt from *Alice's Adventure in Wonderland* by Lewis Carroll:

"Would you tell me please which way I ought to go from here?"
said Alice.

"That depends a good deal on where you want to get to," said the Cat.

"I don't much care where," said Alice.

"Then it doesn't much matter where you go," said the Cat.

It was time for us to get better at answering the question of where we wanted to go as a company—together.

Holly helped us walk the team through our trend and SWOT analysis in a way where everyone participated and contributed to the discussion. We broke everyone up into subgroups—administration/finance, customer technical work, business development, and overall corporate functions—to start at the bottom and roll up our forecasts and projections for the company as a whole. Much of the material was like what I had tried to present to the team, but Holly was teaching us her way.

We broke down who our key competitors were and how we stacked up against them. We talked about the contracts we had won, the ones we didn't, the expiring ones we would soon need to recompete, and future contracts we should go after. She also had us tackle questions like, How will we measure our key operating achievements related to revenue and profit? What organizational skills and knowledge need to exist to achieve those goals? What organizational structures need to exist? How are we known by our customers? What are the principles and values we use to guide our behaviors as an organization?

"We took a hard, unabashed look at ourselves," said Scott. "It was like going through an internal audit. Everyone had an equal voice in the room."

Holly was helping us define what our "current reality" would be by the end of the calendar year and what our "destination model" should look like two years down the road. The roadmap between the two would provide a strategy for growth. In other words, it would help us collectively answer the question of who we wanted to be when we "grew up" as a company, and provide a plan to get there. Holly also introduced us to the concept of using scorecards to measure our progress toward the goals we would set for ourselves on our growth path.

When Holly wrapped up her exercises with the team, we had a clear picture of our "destination statement," which was essentially what we collectively believed the company would look and act like in the future. Everyone was unanimous in support of the revenue and profit forecast. And when I saw what that looked like, my face broke out in a huge smile.

Remember that I wasn't allowed to participate in the exercises so I wouldn't influence any of the results. But when she unveiled the plan the team had come up with, their growth goals were just about double the growth numbers I had been trying to get them to embrace.

In fact, I thought their numbers were *too* big. I wasn't sure we could grow as fast as they thought we could. I suggested that perhaps we should scale back some of those expectations. The script had been flipped!

Holly admitted that the revenue and profit numbers on the forecasts were big. She said none of her other clients had ever been so aggressive in their plans for growth. But she refused to change them. "These are the team's numbers," she told us. Two years later, we had exceeded our plan.

A Blueprint for the Future

That was a critical moment in Torch's history, because it was the origin of the strategic blueprint we have continued to use and refine ever since. We really can't give Holly enough credit for helping us build what has become an important muscle for Torch. We did bring her back a few times in those early years to help keep us on track, but we've since taken it and run with it.

Every year, we start our strategic planning process in June or July, and it runs all the way through February. This is a big part of the way we embrace open-book management by giving our employee-owners all the information they need to decide if they should buy into where the company is headed. The plan is then shared with the entire company through our all-hands meetings and in operational groups. Individual goals (used in performance appraisals) are then set based on our corporate goals. Put another way, the strategic planning process influences everything we do inside the company.

Year after year, we have relied on this process to help differentiate ourselves from our competitors. It's become one of the most productive and valuable things the leadership team does together. But perhaps more importantly, it connects the leadership team to the employees on the front line of the business because that's where the data and the expertise to fill out an accurate SWOT comes from. By making the process inclusive and as bottom-up instead of top-down as possible, we could get buy-in in a way that I could never do when everyone thought it was just "Bill's Plan."

Work Hard, Play Hard

In September 2009, we took the leadership team to an off-site meeting in Chattanooga, Tennessee, to revisit our strategic plan. This was also a chance to welcome one of our newest recruits, John Watson, whom I had known back in my Nichols days. I had tried hard to get John to join Torch ever since we started. But it took a series of events to finally make it happen—including landing those big new contracts. John was a master of business development and we were going to need his skills to keep the company growing.

It was becoming standard practice at these off-site events for me to sit down with the spouses of our leadership team to give them the chance to ask questions and perhaps even complain a bit. We then followed this up with a nice meal out for everyone. As much as we worked hard, we also liked to play hard.

The year we were in Chattanooga, we had booked The Foundry for our dinner. It was a fancy place, four-stars, but it also had a pool table. At the time, we had an open bar policy for everyone, and boy, did people take advantage.

As the evening went on, and as more and more bottles of wine were opened and sipped, things started to get a bit out of hand—some of which I helped provoke.

Sitting on the table in front of me was one of the corks from a bottle. Someone (I don't remember who) bet me that I couldn't hit Terry Thomas, who was sitting across the table from us, with that cork. Never one to shy away from a challenge, I flicked my wrist and—*Whap!*—that cork hit Terry square between the eyes.

Terry had no idea who had thrown the cork. So, as he scanned the room for the culprit, he took the cork and let it fly at someone else. Only, the cork ricocheted and—*Plop!*—landed right in John Watson's wineglass.

At that point, other corks and maybe even some bread rolls started flying around the room. We had started a full-on food fight.

For his part, John began to clamp his hand down over his wineglass anytime he spied something sailing through the air.

"I thought to myself, my Lord, what have I gotten myself into," said John.[16]

It was, admittedly, a mess, and our HR director at the time had a bit of a breakdown over it as she tried to get us to stop.

When I went to settle the bill with the waiter (the check total was *enormous*), I made sure to give him a healthy tip to make up for the mess and the ruckus. But do you know what he told me? He thanked me. He said that he and his staff had so much fun serving us, and they wanted to present us with a bottle of wine—the most expensive one they had.

Strangely enough, it always seemed like Terry Thomas was involved when things crossed a line. I'll never forget how, at another off-site meeting, Terry went looking for his eyeglasses that he misplaced, only to find them sitting on the head of a lobster on a seafood platter.

I guess what we proved is that we all were working hard— really hard—to grow our company. And one of the ways we dealt with the high levels of stress was to let loose every now and again, making many memories that will not be soon forgotten.

---

16. John Watson, in conversation with the author, August 10, 2022.

CHAPTER NINE

Embracing Growth and Expansion

S tarting in 2011, the year that Torch became 100 percent employee-owned by its ESOP, we also began another rocket ship ride of growth and expansion. The fruits of hard work through our strategic planning process and our commitment to becoming a growth company began to pay off.

The first significant leap came in March 2011, when we landed our first major contract to work with the Missile Defense Agency. The Missile Defense Agency Engineering and Support Services (MiDAESS) contract came with a potential ceiling of $861 million, which could be realized only by winning task order competitions. The MiDAESS contract came with a very significant new rule: All subcontractors had to be exclusive to their MiDAESS primes for all task order bids. The Torch team had significant incumbency on only one of the planned ten task orders on MiDAESS. Thus, the rational business decision would be to bid only that one task order. However, across our team, we had small amounts of incumbency in every one of the ten task orders. Those incumbent subcontractors were, by rule of the government, forced to only be on the Torch team. Thus, if we did not bid, then those incumbent employees would have to leave their current company and join the winning company if they wanted to continue the work. This was a dilemma.

In the end, we decided we had to bid on all ten. It was the right thing to do—we had to at least try for the sake of our teammates. As it turned out, Torch won five of the ten task orders, which represented two-thirds of the work (competing against four other MiDAESS primes).

At the time, we had 160 or so employees—all but two of whom worked in Huntsville. John was executing on the mission we gave him when he joined as head of our business development efforts. In the early days of the company, it didn't make much sense to look outside of Huntsville because most of us were working on-site with our customers there. But I was excited to see us plant our flag elsewhere.

John understood how we used our strategic planning process to systematically evaluate different markets and see how we matched up with them. He was better at it than I was. Once we got the recipe going, we were able to build on that and start other locations. "We weren't trying to grow for growth's sake," said John, "only where we thought it made the most sense for us."

In 2013, we bid and won a $9 million, three-year contract in Eglin, Florida, for Gulf Range Drone Control System (GRDCS), a US Air Force project. This was our first major prime contract win that did not involve our Huntsville customers.

An Expanding Footprint

Bidding on—and winning—that Air Force contract in Florida was a perfect example of the culture of employee-ownership we were building at Torch. This was based on a relationship John Watson had nurtured for years and involved similar work that we had been doing for the US Army. If we won this bid, it would mean staffing up our relatively new field office in Eglin. But we needed our current team leads and project managers to tackle the work to win the proposal. The catch was that we needed to ask people to do the backbreaking proposal work even though they and their teams wouldn't directly benefit. We didn't want to beg or force them; they needed to want to do the work voluntarily. They needed to see that winning that contract was something they would benefit from because it would help grow the company and the ESOP.

In the end, after many long nights and weekends, we did win that contract, and the company became stronger and more diversified in terms of our customer base and contracts than ever before. We also continued to reinforce the culture we were building that encouraged people from different areas of the company to work cooperatively with a larger goal in mind: building the value of the business, together.

As Torch continued to grow our footprint, our reputation was growing as well, which helped us win new contracts and recruit talented employees. In April 2013, we opened a field office in Colorado Springs, Colorado, followed by a new office in Shalimar, Florida, in July 2014. As of this writing, Torch now has eighteen different offices, and 30 percent of our employee-owners are based outside of Huntsville.

That's humbling to think about and look back on. When Don and I first met to scratch out the idea for Torch, we had hoped to maybe hire a hundred employees. While both Don and I had plenty of experience opening and running field offices at Nichols Research, I'm not sure we ever thought we would expand to locations around the country, much less the world. I can't wait to see where things might end up after another twenty years.

Recognition and Rewards

This period of expansion was also when Torch began to earn even more recognition as a special place to work. In 2011, we were named to *Inc.* magazine's list of Winning Workplaces, and in 2012, the National Center for Employee Ownership (NCEO) bestowed us the Innovation in Employee Ownership award for the wild success of our Torch Helps program. In 2013, we were named Southeast Regional Small Business Prime Contractor of the Year by the US Small Business Administration—something we remain proud of even today.

Growth Pains

There can be a downside to growth, as well. We realized there was a price to pay if we lost focus on our priorities. In 2013, for example, we had to rally the team together to recompete those prime contract task orders we had won back in 2008. As it turned out, the MiDAESS task orders were also up for bids again. In other words, we were essentially rebidding every significant contract the company had in a single year.

Cumulatively, that set of contracts had put the company on an incredible trajectory. But now we had to ensure we could keep working on them—and it was going to take an incredible amount of work and stress to make it happen.

"This was going to be the biggest proposal year in terms of paper volume the company had ever done," said Clay Hagan, noting it was going to take fifteen times the people and ten times the effort than what it took us back in 2008.[17]

Things became more complicated when the government opened up a new opportunity called OASIS (as opposed to the EXPRESS contracts we had already won) that promised to change how we would bid on contracts from that point on. It was unclear, though, if this would become the new standard or

---

17. Clay Hagan, in conversation with the author, August 15 and August 22, 2022.

not. We had some debate among the team about whether we had the manpower to complete the proposals on the recompete bids, do the work needed to compete on contracts covered by OASIS in the future, and bid a growth proposal called D3I that we had been following for more than two years.

Clay was one of the people caught in the middle. He had played an instrumental role in helping us win those initial contracts and worked hard on all the recompete proposals. However, he also believed we couldn't afford to pass on the work needed for OASIS. But there weren't enough hours in a day for him to lead both OASIS and D3I. He needed to be allocated to one effort or the other.

In the end, we had Clay chase the OASIS bid—which wound up as yet another example of Torch Luck. What we didn't know at the time was how OASIS would eventually become the standard any company needed to pass if they wanted to bid as a prime contractor. The Air Force was the first to commit to it, but by 2016, it was the new standard. Thanks to the superhuman efforts of Clay and others, Torch was in a prime position to win contracts in the years to come. As it turned out, we also won D3I, and the superhuman efforts of Jim Braswell on the D3I proposal made him a rising star in Torch.

Sticking to Our Principles

Not everything worked out as we intended during this time. In 2013, even as the entire company rallied together, we suffered our first loss of a recompeted contract with our air and missile defense customer. This was devastating. It was the first major contract we had ever won, and it involved the same team of employees who helped start Torch. These were folks with single-digit employee numbers. They were family. Traditionally when situations like this happen, the company who wins the bid recruits and hires away those employees the customer values the most. We refused to let that happen.

Looking back, I think we had become complacent and took things for granted. Our customer had been sending us clues, but we had somehow ignored the message. It became an abrupt wake-up call.

But as we had done a few years earlier, we pledged to keep everyone on the payroll. We let everyone know they were part of our family and owners of the company, and we would find work for them to do. We were all in this to build something together.

Expanding the Company's Reach

When we made the final payment in 2014 on the debt that enabled the ESOP to purchase the entire company on behalf of the employee-owners, Torch had a new opportunity. We had cash we needed to put to work. As a 100 percent ESOP-owned S-Corp, we didn't pay any income taxes—which was like adding 40 percent to our bottom line. And now that we had paid off our debt, we started to look at where we could redeploy that cash.

One area I had in mind was finding where we could cover

the repurchase liability on the ESOP. In other words, we needed to find ways to generate enough money to cover the shares in the ESOP, should our employee-owners want to retire. This is an area many ESOP companies overlook, and it forces them to make decisions like selling the company. That was the last thing we wanted to do.

But the value of Torch was growing something like 30 percent a year, while we were earning 1 percent in the bank. We needed to find a way to generate a greater return on our money to help cover our repurchase liability. We had considered making acquisitions with our war chest of cash. But we were also in a delicate position; we didn't want to significantly expand our headcount because, in terms of the types of government contracts we could bid on, we were still considered a small business. That wasn't a line we were ready to cross—at least not yet.

Eventually, we hit upon the idea that real estate might be the kind of business that met our criteria for generating a good return without adding a significant number of employees. But for us to even consider buying buildings, we needed to create a different corporate structure. If we owned our own building, for example, we couldn't be reimbursed by the government for any rent or facility expenses. At the same time, we wanted the ESOP to have the upside of owning any buildings we purchased, as opposed to someone like me or an outside real estate tycoon owning them.

A first step we took in solving this was to reorganize the company by creating a new entity, Starfish Holdings, which would serve as the parent company for Torch Technologies and any real estate we might buy or other companies we might start or acquire in the future. I liked the name because even when a starfish loses an arm, it can regrow a new one. It's built to survive—just like Torch would be.

Moving On Up

Ever since Don and I started the company, we have always faced the pressure of running out of space. I can look back and smile as I see the progression of offices we occupied over the years: from the back of the First Commercial Bank, to a small office park in a bad part of town, to an office on Drake Street. It seemed like every place we moved into we immediately grew out of. And that was with many of our employees working on-site at the Arsenal with our customers. Our growth was outstripping even my wildest forecasts.

By 2005, we had landed back where a lot of the foundation for Torch was laid. We leased space in a building previously owned by Nichols Research, where Don and I had worked.

At the time, there were two buildings standing next to each other. They had a bluish tint to them, so they earned the nickname of the "flashcube" buildings because they looked like the accessories you used to screw into old Polaroid cameras. It was a bit strange to be back where I spent the early part of my career, but the offices were closer than ever to our customer, which was a plus.

But the buildings had begun to age; they hadn't been

updated in decades. Plus, the sister building to ours, Building One (we were in Building Two), now stood vacant. You didn't feel the energy in the neighborhood that used to be there. That got me dreaming about how it might be nice to have a view of the lake, like Adtran and other companies based in Huntsville's Cummings Research Park did. That's where many other government contractors called home, and it made sense for Torch to be based there, as well. We started the process of scoping out some land inside the park. We even hired an architect to do some preliminary drawings for us. We were ready to move to the big time.

We invited over Huntsville Mayor Tommy Battle, and told him about our plans to move Torch out of south Huntsville. He told me he was worried that without Torch, the area would become even worse than it already was. The flight of businesses would only continue, leaving a blighted area behind. While we occupied one of the former Nichols buildings, the other one had been vacant for years. "I'm afraid if you leave, those buildings will never light up again," the mayor told me. He wanted to know what it would take for us to stay where we were.

I chuckled and let the mayor know that what I really wanted was a view of that lake from my office window. I wasn't alone in having my heart set on moving to the research park. To his credit, the mayor didn't give up. He kept pressing. When I told him we were going to get huge incentives from the city to move into the research park, he said he'd match them if we stayed. "We need someone to make the commitment to rebuild south Huntsville," the mayor told me.

When he said that, he hit a nerve. He was right. If Torch moved its offices away, this part of the community would suffer. I had to make the best possible decision for the future of the company and our employee-owners; but at the same time, our community was very important to us.

A Bold New Vision

If we were going to make the decision to stay where we were, I decided it would only make sense if we owned both buildings. We were paying a significant amount of rent that we could save and instead turn into an investment for the employee-owners. We could create a research park of our own.

I had seen Nichols attempt something similar when I still worked there—and it didn't pan out well. Mixing a defense contractor with a commercial venture, such as owning real estate, was a disaster waiting to happen. In fact, it was one of the many things that eventually forced Nichols to sell.

We had an advantage working for us: Starfish. We could put a holding company in place, then we could start a new business that would own the real estate but also operate entirely separately from the core contracting business. The more I analyzed the issue, the more it began to add up in favor of doing this. What really got me excited was the idea of using real estate holdings as a kind of hedge against the repurchase liability of the ESOP. If we ever got into trouble with liquidity (having enough cash on hand) we could either borrow against the buildings or, worst-case, sell them to generate cash.

But I wasn't entirely sure the board would agree to the plan. I knew some of the board members were skeptical. It was a foreign concept for us to start a different business that would then own the real estate we worked in. As fate would have it, the day I planned to make my official pitch to the board to move ahead with purchasing the building, an article came out in the *Wall Street Journal* about the grocery chain Publix. Like Torch, Publix was owned by an ESOP, and the article was about how Publix had begun buying up its buildings. That went a long way in convincing them to give me the thumbs up to move ahead.

If we were going to make this bold bet, we were going to go all in and make our research park. But we couldn't get ahead of ourselves. We first needed to see what it was going to cost us to buy the building we occupied, as well as its twin next door.

When I called up the property's owner and asked what they would sell Building One for, the gentleman on the other end of the line said $3.9 million. I laughed—that was an outrageous price. I counter-offered with $1 million. Now, it was his turn to laugh. We seemed to be at an impasse.

So, I called up the mayor and told him the situation. I explained that Building One hadn't been updated in years, and it was going to require a significant investment to modernize it to meet our needs now and into the future. "The most I would be willing to pay would be $2 million," I told him. "If we can't buy it for that amount or less, we can't stay."

"Thanks, Bill," the mayor told me. "Let me give them a call and see what I can do."

It turned out that the mayor had spent some time in the real estate business himself. He went about negotiating a deal, later telling me he laid the cards out on the table for the property owner—if Torch moved out and the building next door remained vacant, then they weren't likely to get a similar tenant to move in.

Apparently, that tactic worked, because we were able to shake on a deal to purchase Building One for $1.4 million. But we faced a similar challenge with our negotiations with the owners of Building Two. They were based in California, and they wanted $3.6 million for it. I politely declined and, after hanging up, called the mayor and explained the situation. If we couldn't buy both buildings, we didn't have a deal.

"Bill, let me make a call and see what I can do," he told me. The mayor then made a similar plea to the owners of Building Two. If Torch moved out, they'd have zero shot of ever recruiting any tenants, which would only sink the value of the building further. Again, the mayor helped us bridge the gap, and we agreed to buy Building Two for $1.8 million. The mayor had successfully helped all the parties involved, as the previous owners would have likely been unable to rent those run-down buildings for years to come. We had a new home, and south Huntsville would have hundreds of employees living in and providing economic benefit to the area.

Now that we had laid the groundwork to purchase the two buildings (which totaled about 80,000 square feet) for a total of $3.2 million, we needed to form a company to complete the deal. So, we formed a new subsidiary of Starfish

Holdings called Freedom Real Estate, which would own the buildings.

Reimagining the Future

After we closed on the two buildings, we shifted into our next phase: renovation. Our first project was to build a new 12,000-square-foot structure that would serve as a unified entryway for the two buildings. It would have offices and an event space, and give us a way to control access to both buildings. The new building, which we called the Freedom Center, was completed in 2015.

In parallel, we started work on renovating Building One. Even though it had stood vacant for so long, we didn't find any mold or other systemic issues. That said, it was outdated. To bring the building up to code, we needed to invest in things like a fire suppression sprinkler system and upgraded heating and cooling systems. We also gutted everything— tossing furniture and tearing up carpets—leaving one giant conference room table that had been bolted to the floor. And while there was no requirement to do it, we also redid all the lighting so that it used energy-efficient LED bulbs. While we never really considered ourselves a traditional "green" company, it would be a smart long-term investment in the viability and value of the building. We have continued to remodel and renovate to minimize impact on the environment wherever practical.

Once the first building was complete, we did the same

renovations to the second building. Even though we didn't have to do some upgrades like the sprinklers, we did them anyway. All in, we invested about $8 million in renovating the two "flashcube" buildings. They're now (in my humble opinion) two of the prettier buildings in all of Huntsville—both inside and out.

Perhaps just as importantly, those buildings are proving to be a great investment for Torch's employee-owners. Not only are both buildings 100 percent occupied—which includes multiple non-Torch tenants—their appraised value has climbed from approximately $40 per square foot when we bought them, to around $166 per square foot today. That's a heck of an investment, and it only reinforces that everything we have done as a company has been to try to create long-term value for our employee-owners.

FOCUS ON THE THINGS
THAT MAKE A DIFFERENCE

When we first moved into Building Two back in 2005, Chris Horgen, who happened to be a part-owner of the building at the time, stopped in to visit me in the office. I had a bunch of paint samples and pieces of carpet on my desk. We had hired an interior designer to redo the inside of the building, and I was sorting through the options to see which one we would go with. When Chris came into my office, he stopped dead in his tracks and fixed me with a look of horror.

"What's that?" he asked, pointing to the paint chips and carpet squares. "What are you doing?"

After I explained the situation, Chris shook his head. "Bill, you shouldn't be working on that. Your time is too valuable. You should be focused on what customer is going to choose you, not what kind of paint to put on your wall."

I was taken aback, but I nodded. He was right. Chris's point was that everyone in an employee-owned company needed to spend their time only on the things that would really make a difference to our customers.

When our interior designer wondered about my choice of colors on her next visit, I simply told her, "Pick one that's pretty and cheap." I could see her face fall as I walked out the door. Quickly realizing I had been too rude, I walked back and explained to her the advice I had just received.

As it turned out, the paint and carpet that interior designer chose are still in our building today.

Freedom Takes Off

But the "flashcubes" were just the beginning of the Freedom Real Estate story. We wanted it to become a viable business of its own, operating independently and separately from Torch. We didn't want to have any issues with conflict of interest. And to fulfill that promise, it needed to own more than just Torch buildings.

As a first step, I resigned as president and CEO of Torch Technologies, promoting John Watson to president. I then assumed the role of CEO and chairman of Starfish Holdings and Freedom. I was basically removing myself from the company I had cofounded with Don, and turning my attention to a new start-up.

As we made new acquisitions in town, buying up commercial properties in underserved areas of Huntsville, I also built a team at Freedom. In 2017, we hired Brenda Conville to run the company. And in 2019, we hired Lee Holland to help grow the development arm of the business. Both Brenda and Lee knew the Huntsville real estate and construction market (Lee came from the company we had contracted to do our renovation work), and they have been busy ever since with expanding their team (now nine employees) and Freedom's portfolio.

At the time of this writing, Freedom's holdings now include twelve properties in Huntsville that cover more than 500,000 square feet. It's a diverse portfolio of buildings. One of those properties was a former Frito Lay warehouse, and another was a rundown skating rink that we renovated into a fitness center. They're both now occupied by rent-paying tenants. We also turned an empty field behind the "flashcubes" into two new buildings—TIPC1 and TIPC2, short for Technology Integration and Prototyping Center—that serve as research and development (R&D) laboratories for the products engineering division at Torch. Next up on the development agenda is a fifty-six-acre plot of land Freedom acquired next to a Toyota plant.

Similarly, we know several professionals in the medical field—a dentist and a doctor—looking for real estate who would fit into other commercial properties we are purchasing. These are great opportunities because they would likely be long-term, rent-paying tenants since doctors, as a rule of thumb, don't like to move once they establish themselves somewhere.

Freedom has also expanded its services, such as helping other clients with their construction and building needs, on its way to evolving into a full-service real estate company. The team is now evaluating potential properties outside of Huntsville—and potentially, even outside Alabama. Freedom has expanded its holdings so fast that Torch (which must pay fair market value when it comes to rent) accounts for just about 35 percent of Freedom's revenue. The company has since earned a place on the Inc. 5000 list four times. More importantly, we forecast that in a few years, the cash flow Freedom generates will cover the annual set-aside amounts we'll need to cover our ESOP repurchase liability. That's pretty incredible.

What's also impressive is that the Freedom team is building a culture of their own based on the Torch model. They practice open-book management—where everyone is involved in understanding the numbers of the business and how they impact them. Cash flow is critical to success in real estate, and this is a great way to ensure that the entire team is speaking the same language and chasing the same goals together.

When I get a chance to speak to employees at Torch—especially younger ones who might be new to the company—I encourage them to load up their parents in their car and drive them around town to show them the different buildings that they—as employee-owners in Starfish, Freedom, and Torch—own. They can brag to their folks that they are real estate tycoons!

I'll also admit that it's been a surreal journey for me. As I sat at my desk writing this book, I would look out the window, where I could see the growing Torch campus and all its employee-owners streaming in and out. It would then hit me that I was sitting inside the building that used to be the headquarters for Nichols, where I'd thought I would work until the end of my career, earning a gold watch for retirement. But it didn't turn out that way. Rather, here I was, sitting in Chris Horgen's old Nichols office—now the headquarters of Torch Technologies. That was a pretty awesome feeling.

CHAPTER TEN

A Track Record of Achievement

When Don and I scratched out our vision for Torch, our priority was to build the kind of company we always wanted to work for—and that others would want to work for as well. I'm not sure either of us could have ever imagined how well we would fulfill that dream, building the kind of employee-owned culture that would win awards, give millions of dollars to our community and noble causes, and become the reason people would come from around the world to work with us. Don and I couldn't be prouder of the people who have built Torch with us.

But what sometimes gets lost in the storytelling are the technological achievements made by Torch's employee-owners aimed at protecting our warfighters and doing what we can to make sure they return home safely from their missions. Of course, much of the work we do is sensitive and not easily shared with the public. For instance, I began my career working on testing missile systems—which were like the first contracts we started the company with.

Torch continues to perform high-quality work on missiles and missile defense systems for our customers in the military to this very day, some of which are now being put to the test on the battlefields in Ukraine. It's not bragging to say that we have many of the world's leading missile systems experts working at Torch today.

The key to our long-term success is that the work we tackle is always about trying to solve our customers' problems in a cost-effective way. When we do that well, we build trust. Our work also involves plenty of acronyms—which can confuse just about anyone not familiar with them. Part of that results from the fact that the military loves an acronym. Even though we need to tread carefully in what we can share (and what we can't), I couldn't imagine writing a book about the history of Torch without at least touching on some of the remarkable work our team has done over the years. From implementing groundbreaking technology to saving costs and solving problems through reverse engineering and prototyping, we have always prioritized doing what's right for our customers and the warfighter.

So, I'd like to celebrate the incredible hard work and dedication of our Torch employee-owners by sharing a few of the stories that have stood out over our first twenty years—all of which made our informal Top Twenty Technical Accomplishments list that we shared with everyone as part of our twentieth-anniversary celebrations in October 2022.

"All companies have smart people who do innovative things," Joe Hill, Torch's chief technology officer who helped put together our Top Twenty list, said. "That's now what sets you apart. It's doing something impactful for the customer and the warfighter. As a favorite quote of mine says, 'Discovery is seeing what everyone is seeing and thinking what no one else has thought.'"

Common Sense Rules

One of the stories I love to share that shows how smart Torch engineers are doesn't even feature any technology. It's quite the opposite. When engineers encounter a tough problem, it can be tempting to design a whiz-bang sophisticated solution. That makes sense because that's what engineers love to do, even if it's not always in the customer's best interest. After all, whiz-bang solutions can get awfully expensive quickly. That's why the most impactful solution is sometimes the simplest one.

Early in Torch's history, we worked on a key missile system for the military. But there was an issue: The stockpile of these missile launchers began to rust out over time. The issue arose because the launchers encountered saltwater mist when they were transported on ships. The launchers were designed for land use, not with saltwater mist in mind. When they rusted, they needed to be scrapped or refurbished, which was extremely expensive. We're talking millions of dollars in replacements. When the manufacturer of these launchers said they couldn't find a way to solve the problem, Torch got the call. "Can you help?"

If you were an engineer starting with a blank whiteboard, you might redesign everything from the ground up, to help deal with moisture management in a different and novel way. But the Torch engineering team of Anita Wood and Brian Watson recognized that the best way to keep the launchers from rusting was to keep the moisture away in the first place. They recommended wrapping the launchers in "vapor barriers" (plastic bags, essentially) during transportation and storage. It was an elegant and simple solution to a big problem—one that has saved the military perhaps hundreds of millions of dollars in the fifteen or so years since they began wrapping their launchers.

Flying High

One of the contracts that put Torch's growth on a new, sky-high trajectory early in its history involved winning a contract to help develop systems that would allow fighter jets to fly unmanned patrols over the Gulf of Mexico. This was well before drone technology existed as we know it today. This was work we won in a full-and-open competition, and right off the bat, we had to solve some tricky technical challenges involving transferring data in real time to help ensure those planes could be flown accurately and safely.

This was a great example of the kind of work the Torch team would tackle again and again over the years: solving problems that stymied contractors. Over time, Torch has developed a strong reputation as a team that can solve those thorny problems in a timely and cost-effective manner. From developing simulation and testing systems to help measure performance or characteristics like blast radius, to finding a way to autonomously fuel unmanned aircraft in remote locations, Torch has been at the forefront of developing technology that continues to help keep our warfighters safe.

Getting Our Hands Dirty

Building on that theme of finding solutions where others have failed, we have continued to serve our customers in a variety of ways—sometimes in ways that show how truly ingenious our employee-owners are.

A favorite example of mine involves our product engineering team, led by Brady Porter. A customer called up Brady's team with a really challenging problem involving a critical radar system that dated back to the 1960s. The power monitoring units in these radars were failing, and the military was running out of spares. They had turned to several other large contractors to come up with a solution, without success. That's when the Torch team entered the picture.

Because the components of the system were so old, no one knew how they worked. Our team set about reverse engineering them to understand them better. They even made a trip to

Seattle, Washington, to the technology museums made possible by Paul G. Allen, one of the cofounders of Microsoft and a philanthropist who shared technology with the world. As of this writing, the experimental venue the Living Computer Museum has closed. But earlier, Paul Allen's technology museums were some of the only places in the country where the Torch team could research the components that weren't in use. If the team couldn't find a part off the shelf, they had the kinds of machines at their disposal with which they could build it from scratch.

After this inspirational visit, the Torch team then built an extender unit, which they attached to the units to measure the signals they emitted. By collecting this data, they could understand which signal did what, and then replicate that functionality in new parts that could be swapped in for the ancient ones. The team did their analysis and built a prototype all within six months. And, when they plugged it in for a live test, it functioned perfectly.

What blows me away about this story is that the team that worked on this was made up of the next generation of Torch employees—they look like kids to me—who bring more new skills and energy to work with them than I ever could. It just gets me so excited to see where they, as employee-owners, will take Torch in the next twenty years.

Looking to the Future

One of the newer areas within Torch is the growth of our virtual reality software and simulation capabilities. We have been fortunate to hire some of the best and most promising talent out there—often going up against the tech giants in Silicon Valley—to help push the boundaries of what's possible for the future.

One example is the development of a state-of-the-art virtual reality training system as part of the Torch Advanced Visualization Lab (AVL) we developed for our military customers that recreates a real-life battlefield environment in vivid, three-dimensional detail. What's really cool is that this system was developed using off-the-shelf gaming components to make it simple and familiar for warfighters to learn with. If they've spent any time playing *Fortnite* or *Call of Duty* (which they likely have), then learning to use these training systems quickly would be second nature. This helps speed up their on-the-job learning in significant ways. We've only just begun to probe the possibilities of where our customers can take this technology.

But this story gets even more interesting. A chance conversation with Peter Stallo sparked interest in applying the same technology to medicine that we had developed for the military. Peter is a world-renowned certified registered nurse anesthetist (CRNA) whose company, Prodigy Anesthesia, specializes in online training systems for aspiring CRNAs. Becoming a nurse anesthetist is one of the most difficult vocations anyone can choose—and the consequences of making a mistake can be devastating. Finding the balance between sedating a patient long enough to endure a surgery but not overly long where their health is put at risk is something that takes significant practice. But as with any training of that kind, using manne-quins for practice can make it hard to simulate the stress and curveballs that occur in real life. How does one respond when, say, an alarm goes off or several red lights indicating an emer-gency begin blinking? As it turns out, a great way to find out is by training them in a three-dimensional system that makes that world *seem* real.

What's resulted from this insight is SIMVANA, a new sub-sidiary of the Starfish Holdings family. SIMVANA was designed and built in Torch's AVL to provide a virtual operating room and training environment that combines the complexity and realism of an actual operating room with the immersive experience of a virtual reality video game. Unlike other simulations that rely on a "scripted" approach to training, SIMVANA was designed using the "open world" concepts of video game design, where each component process is input independently and responds to the user realistically. As components are connected together, complex simulations emerge that mimic a real-world environ-ment. Users have the freedom to make independent decisions but will simultaneously encounter the consequences of doing so. Algorithms simulate patient physiology and machinery as user movement and interactions are tracked to deliver an intui-tive experience for all levels. That enables trainees the freedom to explore, experiment, and learn without endangering any-one's lives or damaging expensive equipment.

I can speak from experience that using this system feels just like the real thing. You can touch, move, and even throw any-thing you can grab with your virtual hands. It's remarkable.

SIMVANA is a great example of how we have been able to leverage our holding company approach under Starfish to make new investments in ways that will continue to build the value of the ESOP while diversifying and expanding the reach of Torch into the future.

Who knows what could come next—but we've built the kind of company that promises to grow and evolve in exciting ways, all of which will benefit the next generation of Torch's employee-owners. Our future is bright!

CHAPTER ELEVEN

Embracing the Evergreen Principles

The term "Evergreen business" and the membership organization Tugboat Institute have only been around since 2013, but it was as if we at Torch had been striving for its ideals from our very first day. Finding Tugboat Institute, which is made up of business owners and CEOs who think a lot like I do, was a surreal event.

The ultimate purpose of an Evergreen business is to make a long-term difference in the world and to adapt and grow profitably for one hundred years and more. The framework that defines an Evergreen business is made up of the Evergreen 7Ps Principles, or "7Ps"—

Purpose
Perseverance
People first
Private
Profit
Paced growth
Pragmatic innovation

Evergreen businesses are led by purpose-driven leaders with the grit and resourcefulness to build and scale private, profitable, enduring, and market-leading businesses that make a dent in the universe. Tugboat Institute defines purpose as having a compelling reason for existing—a north star above all else. We at Torch define our purpose in a multi-fold approach of—

Maintaining 100 percent employee ownership
Serving our customers
Keeping our warfighters safe
Giving back to our local communities

Based on my experiences with Nichols Research, I knew that it was one thing for a group of "owners" to maximize the current value of their holding by selling. But we believe it is a far nobler goal to create a structure and culture that allows the business model to last forever and fairly reward all current and future employees with a share in the outcomes they help create over their careers. I never want to see anyone walked to the door, like I had been, because a company is being sold or going public. We strongly believe that Torch and its sister companies should always remain employee-owned and never be sold.

We also want to be successful in creating value for our customers and helping ensure that our warfighters come back home safely and successfully. The other part of our purpose is giving back to our local community. We understand that the local community has helped make the environment that allows our business to prosper.

Because our values align so closely with the Evergreen 7Ps, it was a no-brainer for our organization to seek out the status of becoming a Certified Evergreen™ business. We wanted to make it known, loud and clear, that our purpose was to build a lasting company for our employees. But when we got the results of our evaluation, we scored a 71 (still high enough to get certified). My peers and I are overachievers. A 71 felt like we earned a C grade, and I wanted to know how we could do better. So, I called up Dave Whorton, the founder of Tugboat Institute and the Evergreen 7Ps Principles. "Dave, how come we scored so low?"

There was a pause on the line before Dave answered me. "Well, Bill, Torch received one of the highest scores we have ever awarded. You should be proud of that."

Imagine that. We aced the test, and I didn't even know it.

Living the Principles

It's one thing to pass a test. But it's another thing altogether to live out a set of principles, especially when something as jarring and life-changing as a pandemic occurs. I distinctly remember March 2020, when the Covid-19 virus crisis began. At that time, there was much uncertainty about how lethal the virus was or how it was spreading. Some of my first thoughts went to, How do we keep our people safe?

We called an emergency board meeting to discuss how we as a company were going to handle things and try to stop the spread of Covid-19. I suggested that we commit to a policy where we would pay our employee-owners for a week off if they contracted the virus. If they had a family member get sick, they'd also get a paid week off. I had done some rough calculations using a spreadsheet, so I knew my suggestion could quickly become very expensive—maybe millions of dollars. It wasn't an amount that would break the company, but it would be painful.

Given our deep belief in putting our people first, I knew it was the right thing to do. I also knew it was half-crazy and not something we could ever consider if we weren't a private company. But if I lost my job over it, I knew it would be worth it. Fortunately, the board agreed with me and helped push through the new policy. The real impact of that policy resulted in fewer cases of the virus, and the total cost only added up to maybe $400,000 as, thankfully, not many people got sick or needed to take time off. But it was a big bet nonetheless, and one I would do again in a second. People first—it's one of the Evergreen 7Ps Principles.

At the same time, we also committed to making investments in upgrading our safety and health protocols inside our buildings. We wanted to go beyond hand sanitizer. At that point, it was becoming clear that the Covid-19 virus spread mostly through the air. We also knew that the airlines had begun upgrading the air filtering systems in their planes to kill the virus (and anything else that might be spread that way). I wondered why we couldn't put something similar into our buildings. At first, I was told that no one made units big enough to service buildings like ours. But we didn't give up. We persevered and continued to make calls. Eventually, we found a vendor who sold industrial-scale, germ-killing, air-handling systems to hospitals. They weren't cheap. But we pushed ahead and made the investment: $500,000 to upgrade the systems in all our employee-occupied buildings. We figured that those upgraded systems would prove effective at controlling Covid-19, and we would also cut down on the spread of cold and flu viruses. We made those big-dollar decisions because they continued to show our commitment to putting our people first.

Pragmatic Innovation at Work

The pandemic forced us to persevere and adapt in different ways as well. For instance, we used to welcome customers to tour our TIPC labs, but that all stopped with the pandemic. Another pivot our people made was to use our 3D printers to create face shields and other personal protection equipment that we then donated to the local hospital. We also partnered with a local brewery, Yellowhammer Brewing, to make sanitizer. We requested other companies join in the effort, and we raised more than $75,000. As a result, sanitizer was available for our employees, and thousands of gallons were given away to first responders, medical facilities, and other organizations in our community.

In the summer of 2020, we faced a deadline to bid on multiple proposals for large recompete contracts. Traditionally, our proposal teams all gather around a table and work collaboratively. But with people working from home or socially distancing, we had to innovate. That was especially true because the rules for this specific proposal involved making oral arguments as part of our bid. In other words, we not only had to get twenty-five people to collaborate to submit the proposal, but we also needed to create a structured approach to getting our proposal team together virtually to make those arguments. That's when our IT team stepped up by creating a customized version of Microsoft Teams that fit our needs to a T. Of course, in the end, the government changed the rules to allow for written answers. The good news is that we won that contract—all because of the commitment and innovative spirit of our employee-owners.

The Secret of Succession

One of the core ideas behind embracing the Evergreen 7Ps Principles is that a company wants to continue operating as a private, independent entity. Or in other words, to persist and thrive for one hundred years or more. That's not an easy goal to aspire to, especially because it means you're shooting for something that exists beyond your own lifetime. To me, that's really exciting. To think that Torch will continue to be owned by its employees into the next century just about gives me the chills.

The notion of building a company that will last one hundred years or more also meets the aspirations that Don and I set right from the start when we made our company employee-owned. We never wanted the company to be put in a position to be sold or go public because the business couldn't afford to buy out the founders. But we have our ESOP in place, and we're moving to become a public benefit corporation by the company's twenty-first anniversary. Both go a long way in ensuring that Torch and all the companies under the Starfish umbrella will continue thriving well into the future.

But there's another secret to creating the kind of company that wins a marathon and not just a sprint: You need to have a deep bench of leaders and a robust succession plan in place. If Torch was simply "the Don and Bill Show," the story might have already ended. But we have always worked hard not just to grow leaders inside our organization, but also to give them the opportunities to fly—that is part of the Torch secret sauce.

Consider when John Watson took over for me as CEO of Torch. That enabled me to spend more time working on other Starfish entities like Freedom. Now, at the time that I'm writing this, we're going further. John is stepping into the role of president of Starfish, where he will eventually take over from me as CEO. At the same time, we're promoting Brad Walker, who used to work for me at Nichols, into the role of president at Torch.

The culture we've built at Torch also continues to attract the kind of engineering and leadership talent that will power the company's growth through the century. A prime example is someone like Dave Cook, one of our senior vice presidents. Dave came to Torch after a career in the Army, where he retired as a full colonel. I must admit that I was reluctant at first to hire Dave because of some bad experiences with colonels making the transition to private industry in the past. It can be difficult for some officers to make the switch to the private sector where they're not always treated with the same deference as they were by their troops. But when Dave joined Torch, he took off his eagle insignia, rolled up his sleeves, and got to work like any other employee. He now runs the largest business unit in the company, and he's had an enormously positive impact on us. Dave is exceptional and provides a great example of how Torch's culture is built on teamwork.

Sharing Dave's story gets me energized because he shows how our leaders throughout the organization get to seize new opportunities and assume new leadership roles higher in the organization. I can't wait to see what kind of new ideas and opportunities this next generation of leaders decides to pursue in the future. But it's also up to these folks to pay it forward, to continue to develop the wave of leaders that will follow them in the years to come. That's how we'll truly fulfill our Evergreen dream.

Torch Technologies: The Best of American Capitalism

The first time I met Bill Roark, I was instantly reminded of another Bill: Bill Hewlett, the cofounder (with David Packard) of the once-mighty computer giant Hewlett-Packard (HP).

I landed my first hourly job at HP when I was sixteen. I worked on the manufacturing lines over four summers in three different divisions. That's where I learned firsthand about their "HP Way," the company's famed culture. That culture inspired the legendary business writer and thinker Tom Peters to feature HP in his seminal work, *In Search of Excellence*, which would then inspire a generation of American business leaders.

I wasn't given any special or formal training in the "HP Way." I was taught by my colleagues working alongside me. At that time, HP had begun its decline. The company had gone public decades earlier and, more recently, had churned through multiple CEOs. Despite that, everyone would share their favorite stories of "Bill and Dave" and how amazing they were, even though they no longer worked there. Everyone remembered how Bill Hewlett and David Packard had made a commitment to building a "people first" culture. They believed that if you take care of your people, they will take care of everything else.

Later in my career, after I founded the Tugboat Institute, I got the opportunity to speak with Tom Peters via Zoom as part of a Tugboat event. We discussed the kind of culture that made HP so unique for its time. I've since found myself gravitating to companies that share those same values the old HP did— companies that care deeply about their people and prioritize taking care of them physically, emotionally, and financially, more so than about scaling up the business unsustainably.

Bill Roark helped build a company just like that. Torch Technologies, which is now part of the Starfish Holdings family of employee-owned companies, was started with a strategy of putting its people first from its first day. Bill and his cofounder, Don Holder, experienced what it's like when an employer loses focus on their people when their former company, Nichols Research, sold out. With Torch, Bill and Don set out to build a different kind of business—one that would generate wealth for everyone inside it and not just the founders.

As a successful entrepreneur, Bill had ample opportunities to enrich himself at the expense of others. But he didn't. He shared the ownership of the business with his employees instead. Similarly, he could have owned the real estate that Torch operated in, which is a common practice among entrepreneurs. But he didn't. Rather, Bill created a new company, Freedom Real Estate, that's part of Starfish and is intended to help support the company's employee stock ownership plan. I once had the opportunity to ask Bill why he chose to make moves like this instead of enriching himself. His simple answer was, "I have enough."

Like HP's Bill and Dave, Bill Roark is the kind of leader who doesn't set himself apart from everyone else. Maybe it's his humble rural Kentucky roots, but Bill would never ask anyone to do something he wouldn't do himself. He's always thought of himself as part of the "Torch Family." Some of his favorite memories come from events like the numerous Christmas parties and parking lot barbeques the company has held over the years. Maybe it's not surprising that more than a few of the young people who grew up attending those events are now applying for jobs at Torch.

That's why, to me, Bill Roark and Torch represent the best of capitalism and American business. Bill has helped build a culture that not only values its people but also champions doing what's right by its customers and their community. From Torch's beginning, Bill prioritized recruiting people who cared about other people—a hiring point even more weighty than their technical acumen. Even in a firm where technical excellence is revered, Bill wanted to create a culture that put people first. And during a time when firms are competing for talent, this culture has become a competitive advantage for Torch.

Bill is the kind of entrepreneur and Torch is the type of Evergreen business we should be celebrating—far more than any venture capital–backed "unicorn." Unlike HP, which followed the siren song of becoming a public company (which business schools, investment banks, and others continue to espouse as the ultimate achievement for an entrepreneur), Bill instead believes the greatest calling a company can aspire to is to become a Certified Evergreen™ company.

Bill's commitment to this—which includes embracing the principles of paced growth, remaining privately held, and putting people first—will protect Torch long after he is no longer walking the halls. Put another way, Bill and the people at Torch have never been interested in scaling up for the sake of scaling up; they're trying to build a business that will last one hundred years and more.

Imagine a world where every business leader had a goal like that. My hope is that by writing down his story in these pages, Bill will help inspire the leaders of tomorrow that there really is a better way to build a business. One that truly puts people first.

Business Plan–Excellence in Technical Services

CONTENTS

Executive Summary

Torch Technologies, Incorporated (Torch), is a Delaware corporation headquartered in Huntsville, Alabama, a high-technology research community, which allows it to take advantage of an extremely well-educated local workforce. The Company is located at 2705 Artie Street, Huntsville, Alabama 35805. The Company's telephone number is (256) 704-8672.

Torch was formed on Oct 1, 2002, to focus on providing superior scientific and engineering services to the Department of Defense (DoD), specifically the Army Aviation and Missiles Command (AMCOM) and the United States Space and Missile Defense Command (SMDC). The following scientific and engineering services will be provided—

- Weapon systems performance analysis to include sensors/seekers, aerodynamics, guidance and control, target discrimination, endgame performance, and command and control.

- Modeling and Simulation with emphasis primarily on engineering level simulations including all digital simulations, system software in the loop simulations, and hardware in the loop simulations.

- Information Systems Technologies such as distributed simulations/data management systems, visualization techniques, high performance computer systems, and network integration.

- Data Mining and Pattern Recognition applications. Torch Technologies has the exclusive license for DoD applications of the patented Torch Concepts data mining technologies.

We recognize that the key element for success is recruitment and retention of highly qualified employees that offer a value added to the customer. To this end, Torch will strive to attract the best-qualified scientists, engineers, and support staff currently involved in the objective technical disciplines and markets. We will use a combination of an excellent employee-oriented work environment, competitive compensation with rewards for outstanding performance, and an excellent benefits package.

Business Strategy

Torch Technologies' primary focus will be to provide superior scientific and engineering services to DoD clients. The Torch Technologies management team has a strong background in the technical services business. Revenue will be produced using a direct fee-for-services model. The early services focus areas will be in the application of information technology for military systems, simulation of those systems, and data mining applications for analysis of systems data and trends. The services provided will include custom software solutions, simulation development, prototype hardware systems, and general technical services. Current management personnel have significant experience in areas that design, develop, and support software systems and simulations in a variety of computer languages and hardware platforms. This focus and experience provide a solid foundation in the development of decision support systems for military applications.

Early focus will be upon contracts for technology development in areas where ACUMEN technologies offer substantial competitive advantages for entry. We will also look to establish contracts for technology development in areas that may enhance current commercialization opportunities. Services support will also be provided to Torch Concepts to develop specific applications and to provide software development expertise and ongoing technical support. We also expect the services to quickly expand into areas where ACUMEN technologies are not needed.

The ACUMEN algorithm was originally developed in the early 1970s out of the Massachusetts Institute of Technology Lincoln Lab, enhanced at Nichols Research during the 1980s and 1990s, then significantly extended through internal research and development at Torch Concepts. It has been applied successfully to many diverse applications. Torch Technologies has an exclusive license to this technology for DoD applications. This technology is described in more detail in Appendix I (ACUMEN Technology: Key Features and Range of Applicability).

Business Goals

Torch Technologies has been recognized as performing to the highest standards of ethical business practice and has consistently exhibited technical/managerial excellence. With these standards and past experiences in mind, Torch Technologies management expects to meet and/or exceed our business development growth goals. This will be accomplished in our first year of operation and beyond by successfully achieving these FY03 goals and objectives in these areas: 1) Establishing a technology niche area; 2) Staff growth and development; and 3) Firm long-term business goals. Each of these is described by the following—

Technology Growth Goals/Objectives

- Leverage ACUMEN license to gain entry to existing contract vehicles.

- Focus on past business areas of current management and new staff additions.

- Emphasize staff development with the best-qualified scientists and engineers currently involved in the technical disciplines focus areas.

Staff Growth Goals/Objectives

- Identify and hire one triple threat person in FY03.

- Establish a strong career program for management and technical personnel.

- Encourage and reward technical excellence.

- Enhance retention rate with a competitive compensation and benefits package.

Business Goals/Objectives

- Establish competitive bid rates and related overhead budgets suitable for a competitive defense services company.

- Gain access to 5 or more contract vehicles.

- Establish a recurring revenue stream > $1M within the first year of operation.

- Establish initial business base to include 3 or more customer areas.

- Submit > $3M total bids for FY03.

- Identify one $5M or more Primary opportunities for FY04.

- Identify and qualify one ($10M) or more Primary bid opportunities for FY05 and beyond.

- Win > $2M in awards in FY03.

- Operate with initial profitability of >7 percent.

Sales and Marketing

O ur goal with this "technical services" business model is to minimize corporate sales and marketing expenses. Early sales will be primarily generated through an approach referred to as progressive engagement. In the progressive engagement model, initial entry to a customer area is gained through a variety of methods, such as a unique knowledge of the customer needs, a unique technical capability such as ACUMEN, or through leveraging past relationships based on good performance. Once a task is obtained, the task manager has the responsibility for identifying opportunities for expansion.

The rationale for such an approach is based upon the strong current market potential as well as our management's superior market understanding, business development experience, and experience in finding the right people to meet the customer's needs. Our internal business development team will employ staff in dual roles, relying on the CEO, president, and task managers for sales. These individuals, while not salesmen by profession, do have significant experience in DoD business development. This approach has shown to be very effective in successful DoD Service Contractors such as Nichols Research, Camber Corporation, and Dynetics, etc.

Financials

T orch currently projects it will be profitable in the second quarter of 2003 and will operate with an overall profitability for the first full year of operations. In our first year, Torch's primary revenues will result from technical services with AMCOM and SMDC. We also seek to establish entry into other markets by leveraging DoD and Government contracts for technology development in areas where ACUMEN technologies may offer substantial opportunities.

We will leverage the technology development within Torch Concepts and will therefore expect no Research and Development costs. Our anticipated revenues and expenses through 2004 are depicted in the following table.

Budget (in millions)

	2003	2004	2005
Revenue	$1.0M	$3.0M	$6.0M
Expenses	$0.96M	$2.82M	$5.5M
Income	$0.04M	$0.18M	$0.5M

Projections are based on the past experiences the senior management at Torch Technologies has in managing large government multiple tasking, R&D contracts.

Cost Control. Torch's major cost control method will be to establish operating budgets and to enforce strict adherence to these budgets. Torch Technologies uses QuickBooks Pro as its general ledger and job cost accounting system, supplemented by our proprietary spreadsheets. Budgets are prepared and entered into the accounting system. The system is designed to accumulate direct costs and record them to a unique charge number for each task level as required. Indirect costs are accumulated to numbered accounts to permit easy segregation of costs among cost pools and unallowable expenses. Actual costs incurred are summarized and reported to appropriate management levels every two weeks. Project Status Reports are prepared for each active task every two weeks, reflecting actual direct costs and indirect burdens applied at provisional rates during the year and adjusted to actual rates at year-end. Management will then take the appropriate actions to insure cost control.

External Fund Raise

Torch anticipates that it will offer the opportunity for external investment. In this investment round, based on the maturity of the company, that 20 percent to 25 percent of the company will be offered to outside investors in order to raise $250,000 to $300,000. Subscription proceeds will be used to (a) pay general start-up and operating costs while contracts are being established; (b) provide a budget reserve to fund growth during normal operational payment delays; and (c) sustain early sales and marketing.

Notwithstanding the foregoing, or the financial projections contained in this Memorandum, management of the Company reserves the right to use the proceeds from this Offering for other appropriate corporate purposes.

The Company anticipates that Torch Technologies' existing capital resources, together with the proceeds of this Offering, will be sufficient to fund the operations of the Company for at least the next twelve (12) months. However, funding requirements could be changed significantly by many factors, including variations from projected development time and expenses and changes in personnel and other operating costs. There can be no assurance that any subsequent necessary financing would be completed or that it would not result in a substantial dilution of stockholder interests.

Management Team
and Organization

Torch Technologies has assembled a world-class management team. In addition to being involved in several successful company launches, the management team has extensive expertise in information management technology (pattern recognition and neural networks), software development, business development, and finance. The directors and key management of Torch Technologies are organized as follows—

Roy J. Nichols: PhD, chairman of the board, and founder

William Roark: chief executive officer, board member, and founder

Don Holder: president, board member, and founder

Roy Nichols: Chairman of the Board and Founder

Mr. Nichols was a cofounder of Torch Concepts, Incorporated. Torch Concepts has leveraged technology developed initially for DoD applications to develop innovative applications focused on extracting actionable information from large databases.

Mr. Nichols was also vice-chairman of the board of directors and cofounder of Nichols Research Corporation, a highly successful information technology company. Under Mr. Nichols' leadership, Nichols Research grew to $452 million in annual revenues, with more than 30 locations, and 3,000 employees. The company received national recognition in *Forbes*, *Fortune*, and *Businessweek* as one of the best small companies in the United States. Mr. Nichols was instrumental in the recent merger of Nichols Research with Computer Sciences Corporation of El Segundo, California.

Prior to founding Nichols Research, Mr. Nichols developed and headed the Discrimination and Data Processing Department at McDonnell Douglas Astronautics and was a lead researcher at the Infrared Physics Laboratory at the University of Michigan's Institute of Science and Technology.

Mr. Nichols received an honorary PhD in Science from the University of Alabama and an MS and BS in Aeronautical Engineering from the University of Michigan.

Bill Roark: CEO, Member of the Board of Directors, and Founder

Mr. Roark has over ten years executive management experience. He is currently serving as president of Torch Concepts, Incorporated. He previously worked for Camber Corporation as a senior vice president. In this capacity, Mr. Roark was responsible for management and operation of all aspects of a $40M/year P&L Center. Prior to joining Camber, Mr. Roark was president of the Criminal Justice Systems Operating Segment within Nichols Research Corporation. He also worked from an entry-level position to become the corporate vice president of the Military Systems and Simulations Group.

Mr. Roark has a demonstrated history of proven technical management combined with successful program management. He has successfully managed nationally deployed IT systems with broadly diverse user communities. Mr. Roark has developed and successfully implemented long-term business plans that successfully sustained annual revenue growth of more than 50 percent. He has successfully established program management guidelines and policies that helped triple profit margins while simultaneously generating market penetration into new customer areas.

Mr. Roark earned an MS in Physics from University of Kentucky and a BS in Mathematics from Cumberland College.

Don Holder: President, Member of the Board of Directors, and Founder

Mr. Holder has over thirty-five years of experience in DoD research and development programs. Prior to joining Torch Technologies, he managed large R&D contracts for CAS Incorporated and CSC/Nichols Research Corporation. As a corporate vice president, Mr. Holder was responsible for directing the CSC/Nichols Army Simulation Programs Business Unit and leading modeling and simulation (M&S) initiatives across several business sectors. In this capacity, Mr. Holder was responsible for the technical and business management of a $30 million-per-year operation. His management resulted in meeting all technical, cost, and schedule requirements.

Before joining NRC, Mr. Holder worked for the US Army Missile Command, working on several research projects. He served as the technical director of MICOM's Fiber Optics Technology Demonstration program. He also served as the manager of several Army Tactical systems simulation and analysis efforts.

Mr. Holder earned an MS degree in Electrical Engineering from the University of Michigan and a BS degree in Mathematics from Jacksonville State University.

Market and Operational Risks

The most significant near-term risks to Torch Technologies are described below—

Contract Vehicles. As a new company, existing contract vehicles do not exist. Establishing contracts that allow easy access to key government agencies represent risk to contract awards and rapid growth.

Competition for Qualified Personnel. The demand for highly qualified IT professionals far exceeds the available talent pool. This imbalance has resulted in intense competition in the marketplace for these personnel in terms of salary, benefits, and working environment.

Department of Defense Budget. As a company focused on providing services to DoD customers, the defense budget and specifically that portion set aside for services can directly impact the opportunities for business growth.

Existing and New Competition. Direct competition, either from existing or new defense could also negatively impact the Company's revenue projections.

Personnel Located in Multiple Locations. Because of the nature of the government service businesses, personnel are frequently located in government facilities and therefore reside in several different locations. This greatly impacts synergistic communication and cooperation between the different organizations as well as resource utilization.

Each of these risks is inherent to any early-stage company. Torch Technologies is a dynamic organization ready to meet these challenges. The Company's strategy to circumvent these risks is to quickly work to establish contract vehicles within the key DoD areas of interest. Proposals have been submitted to join existing contracts. Key issues in being added to existing contracts are being able to offer a unique technology and being a small business. The Company intends to exploit the ACUMEN technology to provide the unique technology and to utilize established management relationships with key contractors within the community.

ACUMEN Technology: Key Features and Range of Applicability

Introduction

This Appendix provides a brief description of ACUMEN (Adaptive Concept Understanding from Modeled Enterprise Networks) technology. It focuses on its generality, which results in a wide range of products and its key features. These features, as identified in Table 1, provide added accuracy and currency of the Torch products that differentiate them from those of its competitors. Torch's core technology, ACUMEN, provides a systematic approach for extracting actionable information from any combination of numeric, categorical, or symbolic (e.g., textual) data sets. This versatility enables the same technology to perform advanced data mining tasks and textual analysis, search and association. This technology has been applied successfully to image and signal processing development for the DoD, data mining applications in the health care and financial industries, and to the development of multiple products in the text recognition, association, and organization domains at Torch.

The ACUMEN Advantage

ACUMEN is a unique synthesis of adaptive neural methods, internal models, and fuzzy logic. By combining model-based technology with adaptivity using fuzzy logic, it is possible to estimate multiple models while concurrently associating data with these models. The fuzzy logic makes it possible for data and/or text samples to be associated with more than one model, providing orders of magnitude improvements in efficiency, scalability, and versatility over today's intelligent systems. Traditional clustering or unsupervised learning techniques associate data with only a single group or cluster. This is not only unrealistic but leads to a combinatorial explosion of algorithmic complexity. Thus, the Torch products are easily scalable to large amounts of data or text, and the accuracy of the organization and association functions are unsurpassed.

The ACUMEN models represent the multiple and diverse modes of behavior observed in complex systems in data mining applications, or it can characterize the syntactic and semantic relationships between concepts in documents while analyzing symbolic data. Non-model-based systems require large amounts of data to learn patterns, with data requirements growing exponentially as the number of attributes or words used in the application increase. As an example, many of the well-known neural systems such as the Back Propagation Network and the multiple Nearest Neighbor-based networks (e.g., Hopfield, Kohonen) require large numbers of weights resulting in the need for large amounts of data for training, making them inefficient for learning. The ACUMEN technology learning data requirements are considerably smaller than those of the more conventional technologies. The ACUMEN model-based approach replaces the large number of weights with models that can be characterized by a small number of parameters. Therefore, the ACUMEN neural system can be trained on a much smaller amount of data than other systems, and as a result of the equations that govern the model estimation and data association functions of ACUMEN, it can achieve the information-theoretic bound, Bayes error, on classification accuracy. The use of internal models is another feature of ACUMEN, which permits its application to the extraction of actionable information and key concepts present in large quantities of stored data and text.

By combining the ability to adapt with model-based technology, ACUMEN achieves two major advantages over other pattern recognition and neural systems. First, other techniques will degrade catastrophically if their training data and testing data are not similar. In order for these techniques to approach the information-theoretic bound, they require prior knowledge of the underlying distributions of the data and the assurance that the training and testing data are represented by the same distributions. This is not required by ACUMEN. ACUMEN adapts its models to the testing data so that they characterize the properties of the testing data. This adaptation achieves the information-theoretic, Cramer-Rao bound on learning efficiency. This is important for the organization or association of text as the concepts present in documents and the categories to which documents naturally belong are determined by the specific documents in the corpus under consideration.

Most text processing techniques use keywords rather than concepts to select and differentiate documents and assume pre-determined categories or use humans to determine the categories in which to place the documents for organization. Keywords are a poor substitute for extracting the meaning of documents, and predetermined categories are an inaccurate way for organizing a corpus of documents as it is akin to forcing a round peg into a square hole. The use of humans for performing the categorization is extremely costly and inefficient. The ACUMEN approach uses the extraction of concepts, and it groups the documents on the basis of the concepts present in the documents. Thus, the definition of the categories adapts to the information in the documents, much the way a human groups documents.

Second, the ability to combine adaptivity with the model-based approach provides a powerful means for incorporating domain knowledge into an intelligent pattern identification system. For example, an ACUMEN health care data mining application incorporated the knowledge of physicians

TABLE 1. KEY ACUMEN FEATURES

- Versatile—Applicable to Diverse Data Types
  - Numerical
  - Categorical
  - Symbolic (Textual)
- Efficient Learning Process
- Model-Based Structure
  - Operates on Large Number of Attributes
- Models Adapt to Data
- Can be Used for Supervised and Unsupervised Learning
- No Underlying Assumptions Required for Characterizing the Data
- Determines Important Attributes that Characterize Each Category
- Handles Missing Data in an Optimal Fashion
- Can Determine if Data Is Noisy
- Uses Fuzzy Logic to Obtain Natural Association of Objects to Classes and to Reduce Algorithmic Complexity

and hospital administrators into models that were used for predicting the performance of hospitals and determining the key factors that drove a hospital's performance. The incorporation of domain knowledge resulted in a more efficient learning procedure. The same type of assistance can be built into a document organization system for specialized applications. For example, if Torch Concepts develops an Organizer for the medical or legal fields, the ideas of physicians or attorneys can be used to help in the initial formation of categories, but the groupings will finally settle on ones determined by the document corpus. The incorporation of physicians' or attorneys' domain knowledge helps in initiating the categorization function.

Torch Awards & Recognition

- **November 15, 2005:** Torch Award for Marketplace Ethics from the Better Business Bureau (also 2009, 2015, and 2020)

- **May 23, 2006:** Named to *Entrepreneur* magazine's Hot 100 list

- **August 22, 2007:** Makes the Inc. 5000 list (and for the next fourteen years in a row)

- **August 2007:** Selected as Small Business of the Year (Technology) by the Chamber of Commerce of Huntsville/Madison County

- **April 22, 2008:** Selected as a Best Place to Work by the Chamber of Commerce of Huntsville/Madison County (also in 2012, 2016, 2017, and 2018)

- **August 20, 2008:** Named on the Principal Financial Group's 10 Best Companies for Financial Security list

- **November 13, 2008:** Selected as Large Business of

the Year in Technology by the Alabama Information
Technology Association

- **May 23, 2011:** Winner of *Inc.* magazine and Winning
  Workplaces Top Small Company Workplaces

- **April 26, 2012:** Winner of the Innovations in
  Employee Ownership Award from the NCEO

- **December 4, 2012:** Ranked No. 2 in Alabama on the
  Inc. magazine Hire Power Award (also in 2013)

- **June 11, 2013:** Named Region IV Small Business
  Prime Contractor of the Year by the United States
  Small Business Administration

- **November 5, 2013:** Presented with the Partners in
  Philanthropy Award by the Community Foundation
  of Huntsville/Madison Country

- **June 22, 2015:** Named to the Washington
  Technology Top 100 List of the largest government
  contractors by prime contract dollars (also in 2016,
  2017, 2018, 2019, 2020, and 2021)

- **January 29, 2016:** Named one of *Forbes* magazine's
  Best Small Companies in America

- **May 17, 2016:** Named one of the country's Best
  Workplaces in Consulting and Professional Services
  by *Fortune* and Great Place to Work Institute (also in
  2017, 2018, 2019, 2020, and 2021)

- **August 23, 2017:** Bloomberg Government includes Torch on its Annual Top 200 Ranking (also in 2018, 2019, 2020, and 2021)

- **October 2017:** Named to Entrepreneur 360 List (also 2018 and 2019)

- **February 23, 2018:** Named Outstanding Mechanical Engineering Firm by the American Society of Mechanical Engineers (ASME) – North Alabama Section (also in 2020)

- **April 2018:** Named ESOP Company of the Year by New South Chapter of the ESOP Association (also won in 2020 and 2021)

- **December 2, 2020:** Named one of the Best Workplaces for Parents by the Great Place to Work Institute

- **December 3, 2020:** Named one of the Best Workplaces in Colorado Springs by the *Colorado Springs Gazette* (also in 2021)

- **June 9, 2021:** Received the 2021 James S. Cogswell Outstanding Industrial Security Achievement Award from the Defense Counterintelligence and Security Agency (DCSA)

- **March 7, 2022:** Achieved Certified Evergreen™ status from the Tugboat Institute

About the Author

BILL ROARK is the cofounder of Torch Technologies, Incorporated (Torch); the founder and CEO of Starfish Holdings, the parent company of Torch; and founder of Freedom Real Estate & Capital, LLC.

Roark has more than thirty years of Department of Defense–related experience. As the CEO of Torch, Roark guided Torch to national recognition as one of the Top 100 Fastest Growing Companies in America, according to *Entrepreneur* magazine, and fifteen consecutive selections on the Inc. 5000 list recognizing the Fastest Growing Private Companies, including recognition as the No. 1 Fastest Growing Privately Held Defense Contractor in the Southeast Region. He also guided Freedom to five consecutive years on the Inc. 5000 list.

During his tenure at the company, Torch was a three-time recipient of the Better Business Bureau Torch Award for outstanding business ethics and was recognized by the Huntsville/Madison County Chamber of Commerce as the Small Business of the Year in Technology (2007). Roark considers employee relations and benefits one of the most important aspects of business management, and he has worked diligently to ensure top benefits and working conditions, resulting in local recognition as one of the Best Places to Work in Huntsville/Madison County in 2018, 2017, 2016, 2012, and 2008. Torch received national recognition by the Principal Financial Group as one of the Principal 10 Best Companies for Employee Financial Security, as well as recognition by *Inc.* magazine and Winning Workplaces as a Top Small Company.

Before founding Torch and Starfish Holdings, Roark worked for Camber Corporation as a senior vice president. Prior to joining Camber, Roark was with Nichols Research Corporation, at which he worked his way up from an entry-level scientist position to become the president of the Criminal Justice Systems Operations segment. Roark earned an MS in Physics from the University of Kentucky and a BS in Mathematics from Cumberland College. This past year, Torch proudly announced that it became Certified Evergreen™, a timely achievement for Torch employee-owners, as they had just celebrated Torch's twentieth anniversary. Torch's Certified Evergreen™ status signifies that while Torch employee-owners can look back on Torch's past with pride, Torch is also looking forward and has committed to finding ways to make 100 percent employee ownership sustainable so that Torch will remain a private company.

www.ingramcontent.com/pod-product-compliance
Lightning Source LLC
Chambersburg PA
CBHW030506210326
41597CB00013B/810

9781632998026